PRAISE FOR THE CIVIL WAR SOLDIERS' ORPHAN SCHOOLS OF PENNSYLVANIA 1864-1889

"Meticulously researched and comprehensively annotated, this volume of neglected Americana history, The Civil War Soldiers' Orphan Schools of Pennsylvania 1864-1899, heavily illustrated with fascinating photographs, drawings, and period documents, is particularly well-attended to by its author ... Digging deeper into his subject, (Gold) removes layer after layer of contemporary opinion to reveal a more sinister, disturbing, and certainly more accurately complex depiction of these supposedly safe havens for the children, beginning with a questionably unethical financial motivation for their existence, and certainly a later ruthless and greedy syndicate co-option of their operation, not to mention the intrinsic political graft and manipulation attending the continuance of their initial charters... a masterful job of parsing through conflicting historical evidence in order to tell a balanced story that bears examination for its relevance today... What begins as an uncontested, popular issue of the heart often becomes distorted by the politics of self-interest, the stubbornness of inertia, and even the simple but profoundly unexpected flukes of history.... (Gold) decisively covers each in this fascinating tale of a warm-hearted promise gone deathly cold."

By Joel R. Dennstedt for Readers' Favorite – **FIVE STARS**

"As the only modern text compiled on the little known Civil War orphan schools… provides a fascinating look into a unique humanitarian effort…. (Gold) meticulously documents the schools' existence from inception all the way to when they were rocked by scandal in 1886 and had their reputation further damaged through partisan fighting. With a bonus story on the tragic fate of the Gettysburg Orphanage… (the book) sheds light on a little known facet of American history, one that has eerie parallels to our own modern society… Gold provides the reader with such an intriguing amount of material, as well as enhancing his research with almost two hundred photos and drawings... great for anyone looking to learn more about the Civil War, its aftermath, or American history in general."

By Kayti Nika Raet for Readers' Favorite - **FIVE STARS**

"…. informative, well-researched text that looks at the original unselfish motives for the creation of special orphanages. With input and oversight from some of the leading educators of the time, the SOS (Soldiers' Orphan Schools) were devoted to turning these homeless children into productive, respectable members of society ... the history continues with partisan squabbling that unearthed a scandal and brought about the end of the program… Gold provides a historical look back at this collapse and is able to explain how changes in American society, due to the Industrial Revolution and the need for skilled workers, caused the ineffectiveness of the orphanages….Tremendous detail is presented clearly and concisely, supported with a spectacular 170 pictures, samples of letters, ledgers, and newspaper clippings… (this book) provides a look at an important point in American history that offers insights into the way education and social services have developed and changed over the past 150 years. An added bonus is the unforgettable story of a private orphanage in Gettysburg that brought the horrors of the treatment of lower class homeless children to national attention."

Reviewed By Melinda Hills

From the Author...

As I was teaching a research seminar to high school seniors, I discovered in the local historical society an old volume entitled, *"The Annual Report of the Superintendent of the Soldiers' Orphan Schools of Pennsylvania."*

Being a research minded academic historian with a Ph. D in American History, I was intrigued with Soldiers' Orphan Schools of Pennsylvania established during the Civil War. I had never heard of or was aware of such a system of schools.

Becoming more acquainted with the Soldiers' Orphan Schools, I realized that it was a topic that had never been investigated by a trained historian. No bona fide historical study existed of the Civil War Soldiers' Orphan Schools of Pennsylvania.

With this book, there is now a reliable account of a unique state philanthropic effort. Much has been written about the military action of the Civil War and life on the home front. However, no account is available which documents the plight of the children orphaned in the keystone state.

In particular, the descendants of the over ten thousand Civil War soldiers' orphans who went through the system now have a resource which describes how the Commonwealth of Pennsylvania educated and cared for their ancestors. Also included are details of the National "scandal" which brought about the demise of these schools, accusing school caregivers of cruel and unspeakable acts.

All in all, I look upon my effort as the filling of an empty niche in American history. My goal was to create a readable, scholarly and amply illustrated history of the Civil War Soldiers' Orphan Schools of Pennsylvania, 1864-1889.

- Dr. O. David Gold

Civil War Child in Mourning

The Civil War Soldiers' Orphan Schools of Pennsylvania 1864 - 1889

O. David Gold

With additional research & contributions by Martha Gold

Also by Dr. O. David Gold

THE GOLD FAMILY HISTORY- *Eleven Generations from Moravia to Pennsylvania.*

NOTE:

Although great efforts have been made to include photographs and drawings that are specifically of the Pennsylvania Soldiers' Orphans, we have opted to include photographs and etchings of the period to illustrate the history.

All rights reserved. No part of this book may be reproduced, modified, copied and/or distributed by any means for commercial or non-commercial purposes unless written permission has been granted by the author, with the exception of brief quotations.

PENDRAGON

Copyright © 2016 Dr. O. David Gold

All rights reserved.

ISBN-10: 1-943293-04-X
ISBN-13: 978-1-943293-04-9

DEDICATION

This book is dedicated to my dear wife, Barbara. She had to raise our two babies when I was away for a year in College Park, Maryland so many years ago when I first researched this subject for my dissertation.

So, Barbara I love you, and will tell the world how you endured the actions of your obstreperous young husband.

Civil War Boy in Mourning with his Dog

CONTENTS

Acknowledgments 1

1. Origin of the Soldiers' Orphan Schools of Pennsylvania 3
2. Centralized State Control 14
3. Justification of the System 28
4. The Schools 44
5. The Curriculum & Daily Life 63
6. Scandal 97
7. Industrialization and the End of the System 108
8. The Administrative Failure of the System 127
9. Politics and the End of the System 151
10. The Legacy of the Sodiers' Orphan Schools of Pennsylvania 170

Bonus Feature - The Ill Fated Gettysburg Orphanage 190

End Notes 252

Select Bibliography 271

Index 279

Street Urchins 1800's

ACKNOWLEDGMENTS

As this book was inspired by the subject matter of my dissertation, I feel compelled to mentioned those who helped me obtain my doctorate almost 50 years ago.

Dr. Wiggin, my principal adviser must have been in her sixties back in the 20th century as were the other numerous faculty members who guided me. But I owe these individuals of the past a sincere thank you.

As to this more recent endeavor, I wish to thank Marilyn Parrish and Janet Dotterer, archivists at Millersville University, Mrs Simon of the Harford Historical Society, Sandra Momyer, archivist of Historic Yellow Springs and Carl Bloss, archivist at the Bethany Children's Home, Carolyn Sautter and Ronald Couchman, Gettysburg College Archives and Matt Harris from the University of Kentucky.

I would like to thank my dear daughter, Martha Gold for all of her hard work.

In addition, I would like to thank the following for their contributions of pictures and artwork:

Kenny Davis, Paul Rodriguez, Rick and Brian, Shirley, Hazel and Ben, George Wattensons, Mark and Gert Hendrickson, George and Carol Marks, Deborah Hampton, Charles Upton, Mary Shacklin, Gregory Haf-lemack, Michael and Mary Swain, Delores Havit, Edward McSwaim, Faith Spiciek, Dorcas Inglemire, David McGuire, Thomas and Bernadette d'Ig-uire, Rosa Marie McClubine, Georgia and her family, Mac McDouglas, The Talberts, The Reese Family, The Smith Family & The Emerson Family. University of Kentucky, The Library of Congress, The Historical Society of Pennsylvania, Museum of the City of New York, Children's Aid Society, Naveen Bisht.

Civil War Girl in Mourning

1
ORIGIN OF THE SOLDIERS' ORPHAN SCHOOLS OF PENNSYLVANIA

There is more to war than the fighting. Who looks after the needs of the soldiers when they are not in combat? And what about the wives and children they left behind at home?

The smoke had hardly cleared at Fort Sumter before the people of the North rushed to the aid of the soldiers in the field. Ladies Aid Societies were organized in most towns and hamlets. Responding to the call, "come girls get your knitting needles," patriotic women made bandages and sewed clothing for the troops. The YMCA sent Bibles, song books, food and clothing to the fighting men. [1]

Relief efforts were also organized for the dependent families of the servicemen. Pensions were paid by both federal and state governments to the widows of those killed in battles. Enlistment bounties frequently found their way into the homes of the dependents. In rural areas farmers brought wagon loads of farm produce and firewood into town for the home front survivors.[2]

St. Vincent's Asylum, 1862

Prior to the Civil war, the public response to the welfare of orphaned children was represented by eleven private orphanages in the Commonwealth.[3] It is only speculation as to whether these eleven institutions represented an adequate response to the homeless children of Pennsylvania before the Civil War. The care of less than nine hundred children in a total population of three million in 1861 does not seem like a particularly overwhelming charitable response.[4] But other factors besides facts and figures mitigated against the relief efforts of the eleven orphanages. With one exception, all were sectarian institutions. This meant that only children of a particular denomination were admitted. Moreover, in the case of some of the Protestant orphanages, preference was given first to the children of deceased ministers.[5] Most of the church affiliated institutions also limited admission to members of the faith from that particular area of the state. The Orphans Home in Germantown, for example, only accepted children from Lutheran churches near Philadelphia while St. Vincent's Asylum was largely for the Roman Catholic congregations of Philadelphia.[6] Four of the eleven orphanages, including the two largest ones, served only Catholics despite the fact that the majority of Pennsylvanians were Protestant.

Moreover, another drawback was that two of the eleven institutions enrolled only orphan girls. In addition, all of the institutions, with two exceptions, were located in the state's two largest cities. They only served an urban clientele. There were no orphanages in the rural areas of the state.

Lutheran Orphans Home and Asylum, Germantown, PA

And what was done for orphans generally before the war continued for the new and special class of orphans created by the war. If they had the facilities, the existing orphanages admitted the soldiers' orphans. The Northern Home in Philadelphia took in one hundred of the soldiers' orphans between 1861 and 1863. During the same time period, the Catholic orphanage in Pittsburgh took in six children of deceased soldiers.

In addition, three new and non-sectarian orphanages were built respectively in Pittsburgh, Philadelphia, and Wilkes-Barre between 1861 and 1863. Altogether it is estimated that about five hundred soldiers' orphans were admitted by the fourteen private orphanages of Pennsylvania between 1861 and 1863.[7]

Again, as with the number of ordinary orphans cared for before the war, it is only speculation as to whether this number represented an adequate response to the problem of fatherless children created by the Civil War. Approximately thirty-five thousand Pennsylvanians lost their lives in the war - probably ten thousand by the end of 1863.[8] If a third of this number had children, it would have meant that there were approximately three thousand soldiers' orphans by the end of 1863. In 1866, an official at one of the private orphanages stated that there were four thousand soldiers' orphans in Pennsylvania.[9]

The first public reference to the needs of the soldiers' orphans was made in December, 1863. On December 4, 1863, the Philadelphia Inquirer described the events of a public meeting the preceding evening in Philadelphia where the governor of the state, Andrew Gregg Curtin, called upon all the citizens to come to the aid of children made orphaned by the war.[10] These few remarks of the Governor seem to be the initial statement made on behalf of the soldiers' orphans of Pennsylvania.[11] This announcement was made at a public reception for the famous minister, Henry Ward Beecher. In his introduction of Beecher, Curtin mentioned the soldiers' orphans. He did not offer any specific plan of relief. All he claimed was that something had to be done for this particular class of faceless children.[12]

A month later, the governor presented a more formal declaration of intention to the state's lawmakers. In his annual address, Curtin urged the legislature to establish a system of relief for the children of the fallen veterans.[13]

These two short gubernatorial messages constituted the genesis of what became the Soldiers' Orphan Schools of Pennsylvania. Until Curtin rose on the stage of the Academy of Music in Philadelphia and until his recommendation to the legislature, no one had publically suggested that the state look after these children. Seemingly, a contemporary was not far from the truth when he later claimed that Andrew Gregg Curtin alone deserved being called *"the Father of the Soldiers' Orphan Schools."*[14]

But why was Andrew Gregg Curtin alone among the citizens of the Commonwealth so anxious to help these particular children? He claimed that his original inspiration came from a chance meeting with two of the orphans. As he later related, on Thanksgiving

Andrew Gregg Curtin

"Ragamuffins" 1800's

Day 1863 - as he was about to leave for church, he heard a knock on the front door of the executive mansion. Opening the door, Curtin discovered two small children, a boy and his sister, clad in rags, shivering, and timid. They were begging for food. They said that their father had been killed in battle and that their mother had just died. "Great God," Curtin exclaimed, "is it possible that the people of Pennsylvania can feast this day while the children of her soldiers who have fallen in war beg bread from door to door."[15] Two weeks later at the reception of Beecher in Philadelphia, he made his first request for help for these helpless veteran's orphans.

The other explanation the governor gave for starting the schools concerned a pledge he supposedly had made early in the war. He told the departing soldiers that the state would care for their loved ones. Now, in 1863, was the time to honor that pledge.[16]

The only difficulty with both of these explanations is that they were made after the fact. They were offered years later to explain actions already taken. The Thanksgiving Day reference was made three years after the episode supposedly took place. His pledge to the soldiers in 1861 is particularly suspect. Supposedly, his promise was made at a military review. But an examination of his speech to the troops fails to reveal any mention of either dependent mothers or children.[17]

Perhaps a clue to the origins of the schools can be found in Curtin's political career. A lawyer by profession, Curtin's political life had its ups and downs. From the age of twenty-three when he made his first try for public office until his death in the 1890's as a US congressman, Curtin was one of the dominant and important figures in Pennsylvania politics. It was 1863 that was his final year of his first term as governor. In his attempt to succeed himself, Curtin faced a determined challenge from the Democratic opposition. The Democrats said he was a dangerous radical, "a fanatical abolitionist" who was seeking to overthrow the "personal liberties" of the state.[18] In response Curtin stressed his wartime patriotism and the voters were called upon to express their confidence in him as he attempted to use the resources of the state to crush the rebellion.

In particular, the voters were reminded of how Curtin was doing everything he could to support the soldiers in the field. He visited them, sent them supplies, and brought bodies home for burial. "Governor Curtin" claimed one political supporter, "has devoted his whole energies to the defense of the Union . . .He has made their cause his cause and gratitude at the mention of his honored name."[19]

As the election drew near, the soldiers at the front would acknowledge his efforts. And so the Democrats were worried about the "soldiers' vote." They claimed that Curtin with his "wily acts of flattery," was claiming to be their "special friend" just to get their vote.[20] And their fears appear to have been justified. Many soldiers were furloughed to go home and vote. And their votes evidently secured Curtin his second term.[21] However, an examination of Republican rhetoric fails to reveal any mention of the soldiers' orphans. His first public statement on their behalf was not made until nearly three months after the October election.

On the other hand, there is evidence that there was a more subtle political consideration at work here. It involved the governor and the most powerful economic institution in the state, the Pennsylvania Railroad. To protect its state owned canal system from competition by the railroad, the state legislature in 1840 had passed a Tonnage Tax requiring the railroad to pay a special tax on freight. This amounted to tax of about $400,000 annually for the railroad. Even after the railroad purchased the canal in 1857, it still had to pay the tax.

Curtin, the new governor in 1861, was an acknowledged champion of repeal and a friend of the powerful head of the rail-

Thomas Scott

road, Thomas Scott. [22] But the legislature that had to enact the repeal was in the hands of the opposition Democrats who cried corruption. [23]

In July, 1862, just after the disastrous Peninsula Campaign, Curtin announced that a grant of $50,000 had been received by him from the Pennsylvania Railroad, to pay bounties to raise troops for the defense of the state. Curtin, however, was afraid that he would be accused of accepting a gift just to protect railroad interests in the southern part of the state. He suggested, with the approval of Tom Scott, that the state use the bounty to establish a soldiers' home in the Commonwealth.[24] The proposal, however, died in the Democratic legislature. But in 1864, the now Republican controlled legislature approved the use of the $50,000 for charitable use, but this time to fund a soldiers' orphan home. More than one modern historian, thus, sees this deal as a way for the railroad and the governor to get the repeal of the Tonnage Tax and still appear to have a soul and be patriotic.[25]

But if it was a matter of reputation, why now did the governor fix upon the soldiers' orphans and give up on the soldiers' home? Perhaps there was more than politics that prompted Curtin to this new ideal of kindness.

Andrew Curtin featured on a Cigar Box

Anyone who has ever had anything to say about Andrew Gregg Curtin always notes a more restrained but certainly more positive aspect of his public career. Political though he was, Curtin is still admired as the greatest governor in the history of Pennsylvania. [26]

Among all the governors of the northern states, none more strongly supported the Union cause than Governor Curtin of Pennsylvania. "The heroic role of Andrew Gregg Curtin," writes the dean of modern historians of the state, "stands head and shoulders above all the other governors of the loyal states as a tremendous wartime leader." [27] Curtin raised thousands of troops for the northern armies. By the end of the first year, Pennsylvania had contributed more volunteers than any other state. [28]

Furthermore, Curtin tried to do something to ease the life of the soldiers once they went to the front lines. A special state agency was set up in Washington, DC to look after the needs of Pennsylvania soldiers. State agents were sent into the field to make sure the sick and wounded received proper care. Curtin

Gettysburg National Cemetery

started the practice of returning the dead bodies to the soil of their native state. And he proposed a national cemetery at Gettysburg.

Curtin personally went to the front lines to visit the troops and the wounded in the hospitals. These ostensible acts of kindness had the desired effect. Governor Curtin won the devotion of the Pennsylvania troops. He was hailed as the "Soldiers' Friend." [29] Even the Democratic opposition recognized the contribution of Curtin to the war effort. "In his devotion to the soldiers, in supplying their wants," hailed the editor of the York True Democrat, "there is no man in our country who can claim to have done anything like Governor Curtin."

Once Governor Curtin made known his desire to help the soldiers' orphans, the actual founding was anti-climactic. In 1864, the legislature gave their approval to aid the children, provided no state funds were used. He could place the orphans in private institutions but he had to use the $50,000 gift of the Pennsylvania Railroad. But in 1865, the legislature gave $75,000 to continue the system. And in 1866, the legislature passed another bill ap-propriating $300,000 for the Soldiers' Orphan Schools.

Finally in 1867, the legislature gave its final approval for the care of the orphans. It set up a state agency to oversee and issue regulations for the private schools where the orphans had been placed.

Andrew Gregg Curtin, who must be given most of the credit for the establishment of the Soldiers' Orphan Schools of Penn-sylvania, ended his official association with the schools in 1867. In 1881, at a reunion of the alumni of the schools, a journalist reported that tears coursed down the cheeks of the former governor as he looked upon the "faces of those he had found in cellar and garret." [30] Every governor after Curtin professed his sympathy for the orphans. Each cited the familiar pleas of patriotism and hu-manitarianism. But except for ceremonial visits, most of them left the running of the schools to their lieutenants who regulated the schools largely free of interference from the Executive Mansion.

2
CENTRALIZED STATE CONTROL

A well-defined hierarchy of officials regulated the lives of the soldiers' orphans. They were real "school men" and not humanitarians. At the top of the pyramid was the State Superintendent of the Soldiers' Orphans. He prescribed the rules and regulations for the schools, approved the admission of the children, and visited the schools.

All four men who filled this position were veteran educators. It is not surprising that Governor Curtin, who had served as the Secretary of the State Common School System in the 1850's, chose similar, like-minded educators to head the Soldiers' Orphan Schools.

Thomas Henry Burrowes, the first superintendent (1864-1866) and James Pyle Wickersham (1871-1881) were probably the most famous educators of the day in Pennsylvania. Both men were active in the politics of a very partisan state. Burrowes had served as an Anti-Mason state legislator in the 1850's and Wickersham was rewarded for his GOP loyalty by being appointed ambassador to Denmark late in his career by President Chester Arthur.

Thomas Henry Burrowes

Both were authors of some note: Burrowes of a volume on school architecture and Wickersham of a still highly regarded history of Pennsylvania education. They both edited the influential Pennsylvania School Journal. Back in the 1830's Burrowes as first state superintendent of the common schools had organized the public school system of the state. Wickersham is given credit for establishing the first teacher's training college in the state. Both men were active in professional organizations, Burrowes serving as vice-president and Wickersham as president of the National Teacher's Association. Today, their names are all over the buildings and streets of State College and Millersville, PA. Burrowes ended his career as president of the Pennsylvania State University. In Millersville, Wickersham organized his traditional school, now Millersville University.

The Burrowes Building, State Collge PA

The other two superintendents, while not as famous as Burrowes and Wickersham, were well-known in Pennsylvania educational circles. George McFarland, superintendent from 1867 to 1870, was a long time proprietor of a boys academy near the state capitol. Elisha Higbee, the last superintendent of the system from 1882 to 1889, founded and had been president of the Reformed Theological Seminary in Lancaster, PA. In all respects, it is clear that the four men who headed the Pennsylvania Soldiers' Orphan Schools were important in the field of education in post-Civil War Pennsylvania.

Two other members of the central department, a man and a women, were the inspectors. They visited the schools to see if the superintendent's mandates were being carried out: the condition of the grounds, condition as to cleanliness, condition of beds and bedding, condition as to health, condition as to morals, condition as to food, condition as to clothing, condition as to discipline, con-

Geo. F. McFarland,

dition of the industrial facilities, religious condition and improvement since the previous year.

The most interesting of the inspectors was Elizabeth E. Hutter, daughter of the well-to-do Shindel family of Lebanon, Pennsylvania. At 17, Elizabeth married a rising young Pennsylvania journalist and politician, Edwin Hutter. He became Secretary of State James Buchanan's private secretary in Washington, DC in 1845. Here, Mrs. Hutter was described as a "star" of Washington society, particularly when her husband was appointed Assistant

Elizabeth Hutter, Wedding Portrait 1838

Secretary of State during the Mexican War. She entertained and mingled with many of the VIP's of the day - Henry Clay, Jefferson Davis, Harriet Beecher Stowe and Susan B. Anthony. But then tragedy struck the young couple – their two sons died of scarlet fever. Her husband decided to become a minister.

The two moved to Philadelphia where Rev. Hutter became the minister of a prestigious Lutheran church. Mrs. Hutter threw

Edwin Wilson Hutter, Wedding Portrait 1838

herself into benevolent work, founding an orphanage, the Northern Home for Friendless Children.

When the Civil War started, both went to the front to help the wounded, even receiving a special train from President Lincoln to go to Gettysburg in 1863. Twenty years later, she spoke of the birds making their nests inside the barrels of the guns now silent. "No longer," she said, "do these guns belch forth fire and death.

307 New Street,
Philadelphia, November 9, 1864.

His Excellency,
Abraham Lincoln,
President of the United States:

Dear Sir:

Praise God, from whom all blessings flow! The Republic is safe! From the fulness of my heart I congratulate you over your reelection. God bless you! God bless your Administration! God bless the Republic!

Very sincerely,
Your friend,
Elizabeth E. Hutter.

Letter from Elizabeth Hutter to Abraham Lincoln

For the Message

Mrs. Hutter suggests that there be four Asylums in each State, own by the General Government, for the Orphans & perhaps the other desolates of this war.

Memo from Abraham Lincoln to Elizabeth Hutter

Northern Home for Friendless Children, Philadelphia

Now they serve as a peaceful home of sweet song." Similar were the homes of the soldiers' orphans. Mrs. Hutter found a "wonderful resemblance between the nests of the defenseless birds" and the "larger nests" of the soldiers' orphans cared for in peaceful homes, protected from the dangers of the contemporary world.[1] Similarly, Hutter's reports are full of sentimentality and self-congratulation.

The orphans liked to see her arrive at their school even for a perfunctory, short inspection: "Here comes Mrs. Hutter, she will bring us some butter!"

In the central office at Harrisburg there were three male clerks who kept the record books and audited the financial accounts of the schools. Here the dominant figure was Colonel James L. Paul. He had been a sergeant in the Union army. After the war as a political protégé of the GOP boss of Westmoreland County, he got the job as the Chief Clerk in 1868 which he held until 1888. His rank of colonel was an honorary one. He wrote a history of the Soldiers' Orphan Schools in 1873. Colonel Paul came under

suspicion in the 1880's for buying into the infamous Syndicate, to which he assigned the pupils. In 1888, he was fired as Chief Clerk. He then became the manager of the Syndicate school at Chester Springs. The last mention of him was a notice in a local newspaper of February 1889. It stated that he was now in California "for his health." He said that "the weather was finer than in June in Pennsylvania with the roses blooming in great profusion, while the snow, 20 feet in depth, can be seen on the Sierra Madre, a half score of miles away. The Colonel believes he is improving in health and hopes to be able to return to his native state to live and die."[2]

One would expect the reports of these officials to give valuable insights into the operation of the schools. But like Mrs. Hutter's piece on the birds of Gettysburg, the reports of the Central Office are very laudatory, lacking any real analysis.

Superintendent Wickersham, for instance, in his report for 1877 claimed that "the past year has been a prosperous one for the Soldiers' Orphan Schools. Little sickness and few deaths have occurred. The education of the children has gone on in a satisfactory manner and they have been cared for in such a way as to make them happy. Of the 7000 children who have gone thru the schools, nearly all are at work . . . many at trades, on farms, or in the professions. They are doing well." [3]

Two years later in 1879, the Superintendent states that "the condition of the schools has never been better. The school build-

ings are well adapted and the children are well provided for in all respects."[4]

Inspector Cornforth in 1879, similarly reported that "the schools have been blessed with remarkably good health . . . The children have never been so well clad . . . As with previous years, the variety of food has been greater. Rarely have I found poor bread. . . The sleeping rooms are clean and comfortable. . . In all the schools, the children are taught to be self-reliant and self-supporting, that all honest work is honorable, and that a life of dependence is disgraceful. The corps of teachers have devoted themselves with fidelity to their work. For thoroughness of instruction, no other schools in the state surpass our Soldiers' Orphan Schools. The moral and religious training is at the same constant as in previous years."[5]

> CHRISTMAS FESTIVITIES AT THE NORTH-ERN HOME FOR FRIENDLESS CHILDREN, at the corner of Twenty-third and Brown streets, will take place, as usual, this afternoon. In consequence of the severe financial pressure, and as there are about one hundred and eighty children in the Home, the Managers of this noble Institution are obliged to make an urgent appeal to a benevolent public, for contributions, either of money, clothing, or provisions. These will be gratefully received and faithfully applied, if sent to either of the following named officers, or to any of the rest of the Board of Managers, viz:—Mrs. E. W. HUTTER, No. 307 New street; Mrs. JOHN W. CLAGHORN, No. 1609 Arch street; Mrs. J. WIEGAND, southwest corner Tenth and Walnut; Mrs. R. HAMMETT, No. 331 North Ninth street; Mrs. A. V. MURPHEY, northwest corner Thirteenth and Green; Mrs. GEORGE DUFFIELD, No. 612 North Eighth street.

Notice from the Philadelphia Inquirer, 1860

Of course, the ever optimistic Mrs. Hutter echoed the positive comments of her fellow officials. "The Soldiers' Orphan Schools are no longer an experiment. It is a successful reality. The money expended by the state for the maintenance of these children has been well spent; in truth, the giving of these funds is the best investment that the state of Pennsylvania has ever made. Now,

I no longer speak of these orphans as children but as true men and women - good citizens of the Commonwealth. Many of the boys are now doing business for themselves and many of the girls are married and now have tidy homes of their own. . . A kind providence has enabled me to visit all these schools. These visits have cost me many miles of travel. Since the schools are located on both sides of the Allegheny Mountains and some of them are 15 to 20 miles from any railway stations and that they can only be reached in a private conveyance over rough roads in all sorts of weather."

It will be seen that the office of Inspectress is far from insecure. "In all of the schools, the educational standard is rising. I was pleased with what I saw and heard at the annual examinations. . . The food is of good quality, well cooked and served. A great improvement has taken place in the table service. Considering the small amount, $25, appropriated for each child, they are well clad. They are very comfortable. . . Taking them as a whole, there is not a happier, healthier band of children anywhere to found than those in the Soldiers' Orphan Schools of Pennsylvania. I really feel that they appreciate the advantages afforded them by the State. . . Finally, I must speak of the noble organization, The Grand Army of the Republic, who feel so deep in interest in the welfare of the children of their fallen comrades. The Grand Army is truly posted with regard to the condition of the Schools and feel a great necessity of having this class of children cared for." [6]

3
Justification of the System

It was one thing to write glowing reports about the schools, but another to justify their existence. Those who were in charge of the orphans were quick to explain the purpose of their task. Generally, the officials stressed three arguments.

First, seemingly to prove that the community was truly in danger, it was necessary to demonstrate that the soldiers' orphans were a social menace. The orphans were pictured as coming from an environment of "neglect and want . . .from homes of ignorance and vice." [1] Fathers were "drunken brutes who abused their wives and children." [2] Mothers were "heartless and disreputable." [3] Most were too poor to send their children to school or find them employment.[4] One widow in York was accused of keeping a house of ill-fame. After it was raided by the police, she deserted her three orphans and went to a similar establishment in Philadelphia. [5] As Superintendent Burrowes claimed, it was a sound policy that indicated "the child's entire removal from the influence of a home thus corrupting and degrading." [6]

No wonder that the children arrived at the schools in such a lowly and miserable state. Most were covered with vermin and infected with disease. [7] Some had no shoes.[8] They were "ignorant, very dull and stupid." Nine year olds still had not mastered

Orphan Girls, 1800's

the alphabet, and eleven year olds were trying to get through the "McGuffey First Reader." Some, especially those from the rural German areas, could scarcely speak English let alone read the language. [9]

Worst of all was the moral character of the new arrivals. They possessed all of the moral deformities of their class - "disobedience, quarrelsomeness, lying, idleness and kindred vices."[10] Practically all used foul language and some were even addicted to tobacco.[11] School records referred to individual delinquents. Two sisters, while attractive children, were "untrue and dishonest."[12] One boy was "insubordinate." Another was known as the "Pittsburgh rat, the most unpromising of boys."[13]

The educators never rejoiced at the lowly condition of their wards when they arrived at the schools nor did they waste tears on the unfortunate orphans. "It is unfortunate," said Superintendent Burrowes, "that these children are rude, very filthy and ragged. But," he continued in a significant and very revealing statement, "these are precisely the evils that the State seeks to remove." [14]

Having proved, at least to their own satisfaction, that the soldiers' orphans were in desperate circumstances, the authorities moved to the second part of their argument. What would happen to the orphans and the community if the unfortunate child did not continue to receive the saving grace of the Commonwealth?

Street Children, 1800's

The word was "crime." Like most educators of the latter nineteenth century, these Pennsylvania educators were fascinated by the apparent connection between poverty and crime. They were convinced that a child of the lower classes, particularly a homeless child, if left to his own devices would grow up not "a plague to himself, but a nuisance to society."[15] They would probably end up "on the gallows."[16] In the meantime, the whole community would suffer from his criminal actions. "Now if the reader will estimate for himself," cautioned ex-Superintendent Burrowes in 1870, "the injury to the Commonwealth which would result if just half of these children were sent out in ignorance and want, idleness and vice,

"Bad Orphans" – 1860's

to some extent, to realize the amount of evil which these schools have protected the community."[17]

To the authorities of Pennsylvania, the facts seemed to be conclusive. Superintendent Wickersham was always citing statistics showing how neglected children increased the crime rate:

"Of the 1,510 convicted criminals in New York, 627 were orphans or half-orphans. In Pennsylvania 516 out of 962 or more than 50% were virtually orphans. In Maryland, out of 537 Convicts, 260 were orphans."

"These are startling facts," concluded the superintendent, "and we tremble to think what might have happened if the soldiers' orphans had not been snatched from danger by the benevolent hand of the state."[18] The point was, as Wickersham argued ten years later, that the state was being spared an epidemic of lawlessness. "Not two percent of them," said the superintendent, "have turned out badly. As of 1881 only one soldiers' orphan out of nearly 9000, 'No A-351 of the Eastern Penitentiary' had been

Five Points Street Kid Gang, NYC – late 1800's

put behind bars for bad conduct and his case was extraordinary since he had only been in one of the schools for a short time."[19]

Further, there was the economics of law enforcement. Although thousands of dollars were being spent on the orphans, this was a small expenditure compared with the millions that the Commonwealth was saving on police protection and prison internment.[20] If it had not been for the soldiers' orphan schools, the state would be spending "ten times over" on jails and penitentiaries."[21] Certainly it was better to spend the money on educating the children to become good citizens rather than for crime protection.[22]

The mention of citizenship brought the officials to the third and concluding part of their argument. The primary purpose of this state welfare program, as the official spokesman reminded their listeners time and again, was to prepare the soldiers' or-

Street Orphans. NYC – late 1800's

phans to become "intelligent citizens and useful members of society." [23] The orphans were being saved not so much for their own sake, but for the sake of society.

"The character of the Commonwealth must be elevated," believed the official historian in 1873, "when the influence of the thousands of children is felt upon society, these reflections, uniformity more felt than the fact that the widow's burdens are lightened and orphans' wants supplied, give importance and grandeur to the Soldiers' Orphan Schools."[24]

Superintendent McFarland said "Pennsylvania will reap a rich harvest from the seed she is now sowing so wisely and well." [25] No soldiers' orphan would become a burden to society as a dangerous criminal. The training the orphans were receiving was ensuring respectful and law-abiding adults. Society would not only be preserved, it would be improved. The careers of the soldiers' orphans would be far different and more noble because of their life in the schools. Here, they would grow into upright men and women.

One official even admonished the graduates of the schools to remain in Pennsylvania so that the state might recoup some of the funds she had spent on them as a special class of children. "We think we have invested in you," said Superintendent Higbee. "You owe it to Pennsylvania to give here your citizenship instead of giving it to other states; it belongs to the state which educated you."[26]

"Ragamuffins" – *1867*

Again, using the persuasive weapon of Superintendent Wickersham, it was all a matter of facts and figures. If less than two percent of the soldiers' orphans became criminals, nine in ten became useful citizens. In 1873, of the 2750 orphans that had gone out into the world, ninety-eight percent were reported as "doing well."[27] Eight years later the results were even more startling: "Ninety-five percent out of every hundred of them become good citizens behaving themselves properly and earning a livelihood by a respectable calling."[28]

The value of the schools to all of society was summed up by Mrs. Hutter, the female inspector. Like all of her contemporaries she knew that the Civil War had been the greatest calamity in the nation's history. Thousands had been killed and even more wounded. But at least there was one compensation for this suffering and death. In a most remarkable statement, this upper class matron was convinced that the terrible Civil War had saved many children from the clutches of poverty and sin:

"It is my deliberate conviction that many of these children fare better under the State's fostering care than they would have if

"Street Waifs" - 1800's

"their fathers had not died, since their fathers lacked the means and the opportunity to elevate their children." [29]

Practically every page of every report contains a glowing testimonial to the advantages of the schools. Some of the praise can undoubtedly be attributed to the desire to defend a system with which the officials were so closely identified. At the same time, there was a more practical reason to defend the schools. Between 1874 and 1885, the legislature passed six acts relating to the schools. Each time the original intent of the 1867 law was amended. These six laws changed the initial Curtin-Wickersham Bill in three significant ways.

Uncle Sam: Go ahead boys, I'll take care of the wives and babies. God bless you!

First, the law of 1867 did not specify when the system would come to an end. Practically all of the later acts set a time limit for closing the schools. In 1874, the legislature said the schools would close in 1789. Later this was changed to 1885 and still later to 1890.

Secondly, the original act of 1867 had specified that only children born before 1866 would be cared for by the state. As of 1874, the birth date did not matter. All that was required was that the father had served in the war and that he was deceased.[30]

Lastly, the later laws allowed non-orphans to be admitted.

Widower and son – 1800's

After 1875, surviving veterans who had incurred disabilities in the late conflict were entitled to enroll their children in a Soldiers' Orphan School of Pennsylvania.[31]

These three changes always encountered legislative opposition. There was always a handful of lawmakers who voiced their disapproval to the proposed changes and additions. Likewise, on each of the six occasions, a few of the state's newspapers were quick to point an accusing finger at those who advocated the increased state aid.

These critics cited three serious drawbacks to the new state laws. First, it was argued that the changes violated the original intent to just aid orphans. Now, children of veterans still living were gaining the benefice of the state. Moreover, what was originally intended to be only a temporary enterprise was being extended indefinitely.

Lastly, and most serious of all, the original law was being changed for reasons bordering on the unethical and devious. The lawmakers were bowing to the most powerful pressure group of the day - The Grand Army of the Republic. Numbering in the thousands, this veteran's lobby was simply taking care of themselves. Even worse, it was suggested that the proprietors of the schools, many of whom were GAR. members, were using the Grand Army to influence the legislature to keep their profitable enterprises going beyond the original closing date. [32]

The defense against these charges of favoritism and collusion came from the same types of sources as the accusations. Obviously, most lawmakers were anxious to prove their support for this generally popular program. Only a brave legislator would risk his political future by offending the thousands of voters who belonged to the powerful GAR. Both Democratic and Republican members of the General Assembly were quick to prove their "gratitude to (the old veterans) by taking care of the children." [33] Moreover, few newspaper editors were willing to criticize a patriotic enterprise that was hailed as one of the outstanding examples of "public philanthropy in the history of the state, indeed of the whole nation."[34]

Finally there was a new source of support for the continuation of the schools that had not been present when the enterprise had originally come into existence. Those now actually concerned with the administration of the schools came to their defense. The annual reports of the Superintendent, his two Inspectors, and the individual school Principals are full of the apologia which these officials evidently felt was necessary to justify the continued existence and extension of the system. Their remarks give a clue to another rationale that was used to explain the purpose of this unique state system of public relief.

The administrators stated all the standard arguments. Although the war had long been over, they argued that the state had a continuing, patriotic duty to care for the homeless offspring of deceased and disabled veterans.[35] But as the system persisted into the 1880's, such appeals were fewer. Memories of the war began to fade. It was more difficult to justify a scheme in terms of a father's supreme sacrifice when one-third of those who had children in the schools were still alive.[36] As Superintendent Wickersham quoted one critic, "Is not the system being perverted from its original purpose."[37]

Street Children – 1800's

A similar problem of credibility detracted from the argument based upon the ideal of humanitarianism. As late as 1885, the schools were being upheld by one superintendent as "a scheme of benevolence without parallel in the history of the nation . . . one of the greatest schemes of human charity."[38]

But such appeals to human need had a hollow ring. They were uttered more for effect than as a substantial, rational argument. They were rhetorical flourishes given without much sincerity. None of the officials, with the possible exception of Mrs. Hutter, connected with the schools were known as sincere humanitarians. There was nothing in their backgrounds to suggest that they

Destitute Widow and Children – 1800's

had at heart the welfare of the children under their charge. These administrators were hard-headed, practical professionals who, for all their statements, were interested in showing that the schools were a practical, not an idealistic, benefit to society. After 1874, it was neither patriotic fervor nor humanitarian concern that was used by those who ran the schools to explain their continued existence. Like a continuing refrain, the officers of the system time and again explained how it was preserving the social order.

Perhaps, it was logical for these officials to think in terms of law and order. With few exceptions, these men and women who were responsible for the education and care of the soldiers' or-

Horace Mann

phans were professional educators. They held in common with the other schoolmen of the 19th century the belief that education had a social utility. They argued that schooling would establish a middle-class utopia where morality and property would be preserved and crime and poverty abolished. The public schools, established and controlled by the representatives of the middle and upper classes, would help maintain the social order. The young of the dangerous classes would learn to take their proper place in society.

The foremost spokesman in America of this conservative argument was the famous Horace Mann. Mann was really worried about the disruptive tendencies of the Industrial Revolution of the 19th century. The introduction of machinery and the growth of cities meant to Mann "new exposure to error . ...new temptations to dishonesty." [39]

For Mann, the solution to this danger was public education. This would prevent the masses from overturning the society of their betters: "Train up a child in the way he should be and when he is old he will not depart from it."[40]

> **BUZZARD SURRENDERS**
>
> **Citizens Believe He is Not as Bad as He is Painted.**
>
> *He Says He Only Desires to Get Free from Imprisonment for Robberies he Never Committed and Intends to Lead an Honest Life Hereafter.*
>
> LANCASTER, Pa., June 5.—The people of Lancaster were startled yesterday morning by news that Abe Buzzard, the escaped convict and outlaw, who for nearly two years past, from his hiding places on the Welsh Mountains, has defied the authorities, was lodged in his old quarters in the County Prison, having surrendered himself to the authorities. Buzzard's career has been most eventful. He is now thirty-three years old. While yet a boy he was sentenced, in 1868, to thirty days' imprisonment for stealing $6. But nine months afterward, August 18, 1869, he with his brothers, Mart and John, was tried for chicken stealing, and all three were sentenced to six months' imprisonment. Soon after his term had expired he engaged in more thieving, and in January, 1874, with his

And the officials of the Soldiers' Orphan Schools echoed Mann's credo. Superintendent Wickersham wanted none of his charges to become an "Abe Buzzard."[41] Buzzard Was a famous outlaw of Lancaster County during the lifetime of Wickersham. He stole horses and chickens, ended up in prison for forty years, got out and became a "fire and brimstone" preacher claiming to have seen the light but whose revived gang robbed the homes of Reverend Buzzard's spellbound parishioners.

Or as Colonel Paul, clerk and contemporary historian of the schools, claimed:

"A few years of culture, when the mind – in a most receptive and plastic state, often gives direction to the whole of after existence. There are reasons to hope that the career of great numbers who were made orphaned by the war will be far different and nobler, for the character of the Commonwealth itself must be elevated, when the influence of the thousands she has nurtured is felt upon society. These reflections infinitely more than the fact that the widow's burdens are lightened and the orphans wants supplied, give importance and grandeur to the Soldiers' Orphan Schools of Pennsylvania, and stamp them as the latest and best fruits of Christian civilization." [42]

4
The Schools

Again, this program of orphan relief operated on two levels. Soldiers' orphans from the age of four to eight were placed in already existing sectarian and urban orphanages.

The officials felt that these younger children were still too dependent and in need of personal nurturing. As Superintendent Burrowes stated, "If a child is ascertained to be unable to read and is ignorant of the very rudiments or arithmetic, and withal is puny in body or backward in mental development, even though over seven or even eight years of age, it is unprepared for the studies and exercises of the advanced boarding schools and should first be admitted to the institutions of the more juvenile orphans... They are managed by benevolent persons, mostly ladies, and several are in charge of one or other of the Christian churches... Still, while according full credit to these institutions, I am not fully satisfied with the arrangement. The children have everything they need in the way of food, care, raiment and instruction but they do not have in these institutions the pure air, the free scope, and the plentiful milk and vegetable diet of the country. Hence the existing arrangement of using orphanages has always been regarded as temporary... On the other hand, if grounded in orthography and reading, and somewhat versed in counting and the rudiments of the numbers, the child should be at once sent to a Boarding

The White Hall School

School, even if only eight years of age. Here, the course of instruction is intended to be liberal, practical and thorough, embracing, in connection, with intellectual education, a complete system of physical training and the industrial instruction... This plan has long been a favorite with many modern educators, and from the experiment, tried with all the advantages of State endorsement, the highest results are anticipated."[1]

But Burrowes admonished the orphans that they were not being raised as a privileged or superior class. They were from "the medium walks of life" and would be raised in the same way as if their fathers were still alive. They should not be under the illusion that they were exempt from "the necessity of labor for their bread." If they, however, showed a capacity for the "higher vocations of science and art," the State would encourage such a development. "But the great purpose," said Burrowes, "is to make them useful citizens in that medium condition of life to which they were born."[2]

The location of the schools was given close attention by the officials of the system. With one or two exceptions, all of the schools were located in rural areas. Although they were named

Protestant Orphan Asylum of Pittsburgh and Allegheny

for the closest settlement, most of the schools were six or seven miles from the nearest hamlet. A few were perched on mountains. Such bucolic arrangements were, of course, justified in terms of fresh air and pure water.

Thus, the Uniontown School, "with due consent of the Superintendent," was located four and a half miles east of the town on the Laurel Range of the Allegheny mountains. "The point selected," said the contemporary critic, "on account of location, being indeed beautiful for the situation, commanding one of the finest scenes in the country. The children are happy, healthy, and have much freedom. They breathe the pure air at an altitude of 2500 feet and drink the pure mountain water." [3]

At Mercer, the situation was a beautiful one and "well adapted to the purpose any could be selected. A spring of soft, pure cold water gushes from the base of Bald Mountain on the east; the west is fringed by a winding stream, the excess of waters from numerous springs. A beautiful natural grove ornaments the property

The Uniontown School

and affords a natural playground for the children. Nature's sweet and vocal systems inhabit the grove and appear intent on giving refinement to the orphan children."[4]

Likewise, the location of the Hartford school was an "elevated one, being on a spine of the Blue Ridge Mountains." The water and air were pure and the climate cool and healthy. [5]

And then there was the problem of the mothers. The officials did not deny the mothers their right to visit their children. What Burrowes and Wickersham were worried about was the effect of such visits on the discipline and lordliness of the schools. There was a highly organized routine in each of the schools. Any outside disruption could, in the eyes of the authorities, be disastrous.

The Mercer School

Thus the inconvenience of the mothers and the annoyance to the management had to be reconciled. Her natural rights and the studies and life of the orphans had to be mediated.

Burrowes seemingly solved the problem in a directive of 1866. The mothers would be allowed to visit four times a year and be housed in a separate room with their child for free. But they could not interact with any other child.

But this problem of motherly visits was neutralized, in part, by the difficulty of the mothers getting to the school. The isolation of the schools, in a sense, benefitted the managers. They were spared much of the interference of the mothers. [6]

And to say that most of these institutions were difficult to get to, is an understatement. To get to the Dayton School, you took the Allegheny Valley Railroad to Kittanning. There you caught the stage coach to the school, twenty-two miles away which left

Pennsylvania Widow with Children

on Tuesday, Thursday and Saturday. To get to the McAlisterville school, the Pennsylvania Railroad got you to Mifflintown and then you rode the stage to the school twelve miles away, every afternoon at 3 PM.

McAllisterville School

And what did the arrival see after what must have been a grueling railroad and stage trip? Either an imposing brick building or a more familiar frame structure. If, the former, it was an Academy closed in 1862 when the teachers and the older students marched off to war. Now, the principal of the vacant academy realized he could make a profit by educating the soldiers' orphans.

Most of these idle Academies were in the central part of the state. A good example was the McAlisterville Academy in the Juniata Valley, fifty miles west of Harrisburg. The substantial brick, three story building measured fifty-four by forty-eight feet. Within a year, another brick building, larger than the first was erected.

The Harford School

The frame strictures were erected by local joint stock companies who saw here a way to also make a profit and bring recognition to their rural community. At Dayton in rural Armstrong County, in the northwest part of the state, the local citizenry subscribed $15,000 to finance the venture. In time, they had constructed three two-story buildings.

At least two buildings were needed since the officials segregated the two sexes. Everything at the institution was done in a separate boy - girl arrangement. In addition, it was necessary to construct the buildings so that they would conform to the standard educational practice of instruction. Before the 20th century the keys to learning was a combination of memorization and recitation. Thus, schools, even if only one room, had to have separate spaces for each of these functions. The so-called large "class room/study hall" was where the child learned and memorized his lesson. Then, the student proceeded to the recitation area to demonstrate what he had "learned/memorized." All followed a lock step routine.

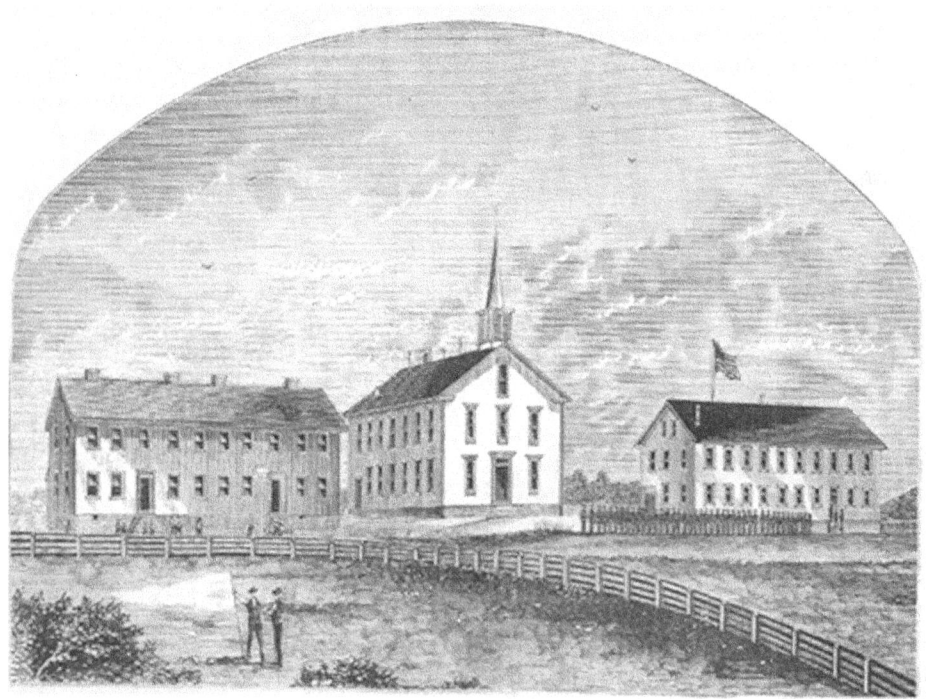

The Dayton School

And once the young orphan made his way to the Soldiers' Orphan School, he knew that he had entered a well-regulated existence. In summer, the orphan got up at 6:00 AM, except for a detail of older children who were roused a half-hour earlier for cooking chores. All were given a half-hour to dress, wash and comb. At 7:00 the half-hour breakfast was taken. Then there was a short family worship followed by play until 8:00 AM when the school day started. At 10:00 AM there was a short recess, then resumption of studies until noon and dinner, again lasting a half hour. School resumed at 1:00 PM with a 15 minute recess at 2:45 and then dismissal from study at 5:00 PM when the evening meal,

Model of the Harford School grounds, upper right building is the boy's dorm -left foreground is the girl's dorm

again of a half hour, occurred. Family worship was immediately after supper and then the children could relax in their separate sitting rooms or in the library. After 8:00 PM, there was more prayer and hymn singing and then lights out for bed. This was the five day routine. Saturday was reserved for baths and play and Sunday for Sunday School and church.[7]

Chester Springs School Girls Dormitory - 18th Century

"Everything is done by the tap of a bell and is obeyed with soldier like precision," said one impressed visitor. [8]

To enforce this strict schedule, there had to be, as Burrowes said, "a sufficient force of employees to supervise and direct the pupils in all matters of order, neatness and work." [9] At the top, of course, was the Proprietor/Principal. Burrowes mandated that this important person, while an educator, should not do any teaching but concentrate on running the school. The main class room was under the supervision of a head teacher, always a male. Three young women, recent graduates of the state normal schools, guided the recitation rooms.

A female matron watched over the girls when they were not in class. And similarly, a male attendant was in charge of the boys.

All of the schools had a nurse and a local doctor on call. There were two cooks, "one who bakes." There was also a handyman and a farmer.

And lastly, two laundresses, one chambermaid, and an eating-room girl.[10] While the Principal was usually a man, one school, Chester Springs, rather surprisingly, had a woman. Eleanor Moore was the only female ever hired by those who owned the schools. And she was highly regarded during the nine years she ran this soldiers' orphan school near Philadelphia: "Ms. Moore was an unusually capable woman," said one observer in 1877, "to whom the trustees turned for leadership when the male principal failed to run the school adequately." [11]

One modern writer has claimed the life of this remarkable lady to be "A Tale of Resolve and Endurance." [12]

Born into a large family in Chester County in 1839, "Ellen," as she was known, was sent to live with three Quaker ladies. From them, she gained an appreciation of good music and fine literature.

Eleanor Moore

She studied briefly at Millersville Normal School and began teaching in Avondale, Chester County where she met a teacher turned farmer, David Moore, who she married in 1859. The wedding dress which the newly married Mrs. Moore sewed is now one of the prized artifacts of the Chester County Historical Society.

The two moved to Philadelphia with their newly born daughter where they attempted to operate a store. But evidently the two were not astute entrepreneurs. The store failed. By now, the Civil War had begun and David Moore enlisted. Ellen and her daughter returned to Chester County and the three Quaker ladies.

Her husband survived the war. In 1865 they moved to Arkansas where they operated a cotton plantation. But her husband died of cholera and Ellen, now pregnant with a second child returned to the helpful arms of the Quaker sisters.

But now her life took a turn for the better. She obtained the position of "matron" in the newly opened Soldiers' Orphan School at Chester Springs and changed her name to "Eleanor." Later, she married Matthew McCullough, a Philadelphia lawyer, and new proprietor of the Chester Springs School. For eight years the two operated the school, with Eleanor serving as principal.

Eventually, they sold the institution and moved to the Jersey shore where her husband developed a beach town, Longport, This proved to be a successful venture and the McCulloughs prospered, being able to often travel to Europe.

But for all her later good fortune, the highlight of Eleanor's career was her sojourn as the head of the Chester Springs Soldiers' Orphan School.

She seemed to be highly regarded during the years that she was in charge of the school. As the Superintendent Report of 1877 noted, "The trustees turned to [Mrs. McCullough] for leadership when the male principal failed to run the school adequately."[13] Her cultural preparation by the Quaker sisters proved to be in good stead. The new principal organized a literary society, "the

Eleanor Moore's Famous Wedding Drew

Census from Chester Springs SOS, 1870.

McCullough Literary Society" which Eleanor claimed brought the sixty student members "great benefit. . . It already is a nice library

Chester Springs School

of about sixty volumes . . . and weekly periodicals [which] furnish abundant and choice reading material." [14]

Principal McCullough seemed to be quite proud of her accomplishments. Supposedly she said, "Although it is tasteless to talk about finances to strangers, I was paid the salary of $1,000 per year which is equal to a man's. I teach the children to exercise, learn temperance and obedience." [15]

When she returned to the school to attend the annual reunions presented by the alumni who called themselves "The Sixteeners,"

CHESTER SPRINGS

S.O.S. SIXTEENERS' ASSOCIATION

Memories

I remember! I remember!
    The school where I did learn
My A. B. C.'s — and other things,
    'Till I was aged sixteen.
And now in after years I go
    A thousand miles to see,
The dear old school I cherish still
    In fondest memory.
And as I near the sacred spot,
    What happiness is mine!
My youth comes rushing back again,
    I feel but eight or nine.
Once more, in memory, the school bell rings,
    The cottage, the buildings, all,
"Sixteeners!" hear the "School Spirit's" call
    Re-une each year, at old Chester Springs.

Poem from the reunion program of the Chester Springs SOS "The Sixteeners"

Eleanor seemed to be the star of the show as described in an article written about the reunion:

"Shy and diffident as a girl, yet possessed of remarkable abil-ity. Mrs. Eleanor Moore McCullough, a former principal of the school, was led to the platform where she spoke in a wonderful way to her former children Though in her 84th year, she used no manuscript and never hesitated. The hearers easily fancying themselves as for-ty or fifty years ago in the old dining room, listening to the clear, well-modulated voice. This was freely pronounced the gem of the day. Mrs. McCullough opened by thanking those present for the most cordial invitation which had been extended to her and the appreciation she feels in seeing that the young people appear to find pleasure in coming together, showing that they have kindly feelings toward one another and toward those who endeavored to assist them in showing them a measure of gratitude for the great sacrific-es their fathers had made long ago. One of the first things she had done as matron in 1869 was to try and make the boys and girls more comfortable. As there was a quantity of cast off clothing about, she had this cut into strips and woven into carpet and placed upon the floor of a room set aside for the mothers when they came to visit their children.

Eleanor

She closed by wishing that the former pupils might have great and good influence over their own children. As the men and women pressed about her to take her hand and thank her for her kind works, she called many of them by name and showed that she held them in a tenderest memory.[16]

5
The Curriculum & Daily Life

Eleanor Moore seemed to have been honest and forthcoming about her tenure at Chester Springs. But were the other principals of the other Soldiers' Orphan schools similarly inclined? Reading their annual reports, they seemed to have been very self-serving and laudatory.

A.H. Waters, the Uniontown principal in 1877, stated that "the health is very good . . .the general educational progress very satisfactory . . the morals are good . . ." regular church service and Sunday school was observed and "extensive improvements were made to the buildings."[1] Two years later in 1879, it was much of the same: "It has been a year of mercies and not a death has occurred. The morals have been very satisfactory and divine service and Sunday school are held regularly. The educational department has made great progress."[2]

Again, the purpose of these schools was schooling and not benefice care. Burrowes set up a rather complicated educational plan which seemed to have been followed faithfully for the 25 year history of the schools. The school day was divided into four two-hour segments. Within each of these segments the four divisions of pupils would be engaged in physical labor or study. Each of the

Recitation Room, 18th Century

three divisions engaged in actual schooling would rotate in and out of the large study/class room and recitation rooms at thirty minute intervals.

His plan is abbreviated as follows:

From 8:00 to 8:30 AM

Division 1 would work.

½ of Division 2 would for 30 minutes recite their homework in mental arithmetic while the other ½ would be studying mental arithmetic out of their McGuffey Readers.

½ of division 3 would be reciting their reading. And the other ½, studying reading.

McGuffey's First Reader

½ of division 4, reciting reading, and the other ½ studying reading.

At 8:30 the whole plan would repeat itself.

Division 1 would keep working; Divisions 2, 3 and 4 would study and recite other subjects.

The head teacher did not hear recitations but confined himself to assisting the pupils in the study of the textbooks in the main study hall.

The textbooks could not leave the study room and had to be used only in the presence of a teacher.

Similarly the examiners heard the lessons but did not give or assist in instruction.

The course of study for each of the eight years that an orphan was in the school from ages 8 to 16 was as follows:

School Room. 18th Century (Public)

1st grade: spelling, reading, writing and drawing on slates, mental exercises in arithmetic.

2nd grade: everything as in 1st grade plus the "four fundamental rules of written arithmetic" with exercises done on the black-board.

3rd grade: everything done in 2nd grade plus geography.

4th grade: same as 3rd grade.

5th grade: same as 4th grade with the addition of grammar.

6th grade: same as 5th grade with the addition of United States History.

7th grade: the same as 6th grade with the addition of algebra and book-keeping.

8th grade: reading, geometry, Constitution of the United States, "natural philosophy of the elements of the natural sciences generally."

Page from McGuffey's First Reader

    Burrowes admonished the teachers that progress would be measured by the oral examinations taken at the end of the year, conducted by the State Department officials rather than by the number of books "passed over."[3]

    The inclusion of history in the curriculum was rather unusual. At a time when the study of history was just beginning in most public schools, it was a standard subject in the Soldiers' Orphan

Schools.⁴ It had two parts: history and civics. History was almost entirely American military history (the battles and leaders of the nation's wars, particularly of the late Great Rebellions.) Civics was, as one official noted, the study of the "laws of the U.S." or The Constitution.⁵

Those who administered the schools gave three reasons for the inclusion of history/civics in the curriculum. First, here was another way to produce those law-abiding, orderly future citizens. The orphans would learn "due respect for their rulers and strict adherence to the law." The study of heroes like Columbus and Washington would show the children what "good character" was all about -"purpose, perseverance, the reliance upon Him who is the director of all events." ⁶

Moreover, this study instilled patriotism. "Pure exalted patriotism," Superintendent McFarland called it, "which teaches our youth to venerate their country second only to God." ⁷ The fathers had proved their devotion in death. Now their offspring would learn it in school. If the Nation was ever threatened again, surely these soldiers' orphans, now adult citizens, would be the first to rush to its defense. ⁸ Finally, history/civics was a way to counter the threat of foreign immigration. Thousands of non-English speaking aliens were flocking into America bringing their subversive radicalism. To counter this threat to the social order, it was necessary to imbue the orphans' "minds with a just appreciation of American institutions, methods of government, and ideas of freedom." ⁹ It was all a matter of controlling America upon the principles of "our founding fathers." ¹⁰ The educators responsible for the schooling of the soldiers' orphans of Pennsylvania would not fail in their patriotic duty to impart through the study of history/civics the great ideals of the United States to their young wards.

Closely tied to the intellectual training in history and civics, was the emphasis upon military drill in each of the schools. As Superintendent Wickersham stated, "Drills in military tactics must be systematically kept up for the boys who are over ten. They are expected to be proficient in the 'School of the Company." ¹¹ Every institution had its corps of cadets who, once or twice a week, went through maneuvers on the school's parade ground. If the nation was again threatened by internal rebellion or foreign invasion,

Boy's Military Drill, Chester Springs School

these "lilliputian soldiers would rush forward to defend the country." [12] America was a peace loving country where the arts of war were "much forgotten and neglected." [13] If the need should arise the orphans would be ready to respond as their fathers had in 1862. During the Great Railroad Strike of 1887, much was made of how the graduates as members of the state National Guard, helped put down the riots at Pittsburgh and Scranton. "The drill they received at the orphan schools fitted them to defend their state." [14]

Furthermore, it was argued that military drills helped instill that sense of order which was desperately needed by all these children. Obeying commands encouraged obedience to authority. Drills taught politeness, faithfulness and the "ability to resist the influence of evil." [15]

Girls received calisthenics as their form of physical training.

But, in the final analysis, it was Character Education that mattered the most to the educators who ran the Soldiers' Orphan Schools. In the March 1874 issue of the Pennsylvania School

Boys battalion Harford School

Girls Calisthenics Chester Springs School

Journal, Superintendent Wickersham wrote a review of a recent book by the famous British philosopher-educator, Herbert Spencer. Spencer made "rash generalizations [and his] ideas were narrow, based upon false theory." As a proponent for utilitarianism, Spencer had little time for morality since, according to Wickersham, the English educator said one could not be taught right and wrong conduct since it came from his feelings. This revolutionary view was too much for the American educator, James Wickersham: "All teachers hold that knowledge and intellectual culture tend to virtue, purify taste and elevate the ideal of duty ...The truth is that moral teaching must begin with precepts." Knowing came first and feeling afterwards. [16]

Here in this book review is a clue to the educational thinking of the men who were the mentors of the soldiers' orphans. Just a few months earlier in the same Journal, former Superintendent Burrowes had called Spencer a "most dangerous and heretical philosopher." [17] The primary purpose of education was summed up in one word, Character. These officials of the schools from Superintendents through the Inspectors to the Principals kept hammering away at morality. "The character built up must be regarded as more important than all else" [18] Reading and writing was essential but for Wickersham: "I deem it more important to train the children right than to instruct them well. [19] To know what was morally good was more important than being intelligent if one could not be both . [20]

Everything that went on in the schools, from the care of clothing to drills on the parade ground, was to add to the formation of character. Character was all important because it was the key to the molding of these God-fearing, law abiding future citizens. Humility, obedience, and self-discipline was what social order was all about. Thus, the primary purpose of the Soldiers' Orphan Schools was non-cognitive. The educators in charge of these schools were only secondarily interested in learning skills. Their main purpose was the inculcation of ethical norms and attitudes.

Herbert Spencer, Philosopher

"Above all," said Superintendent Wickersham, "the children must be trained morally. The example of noble Christian lives must be constantly before them. Every day should witness their rising to a higher moral plane. The end that should be constantly kept in view is that the education of the soldiers' orphans is to make them, not so much good scholars, as good citizens and good men and women." [21] Just to examine the titles of his articles in the Pennsylvania School Journal is to understand where Wickersham was coming from: "Ignorance and Crime (1874);" "Education and Crime (1872);" "Moral Training: Its Necessity (1872);" "How We Teach Morals(1875);" "Morals and Manners(1876)."

Boys march outside Phillipsburg School

All in all, the children were taught to be docile, well-mannered and grateful for their care. These "child-shapers" valued practice and routine for building self-control. Their schools followed a strict schedule and rules designed to promote order, efficiency, and respectability. This ideology was built on the axiom that the state had a moral imperative to follow the values based on Protestant Christianity. The orphans were constantly inculcated with moral teaching and Biblical precepts.

But, it is a fine line between morality and religion. Early on, Superintendent Burrowes recommended regular Christian worship and other religious observances according to the denomination to which the principal of each school belonged. [22] There was no requirement of church membership for a child to be admitted to any of the Soldiers' Orphan Schools. Nearly twenty religious denominations and sects were represented in the different schools: Methodist, Presbyterian, Lutheran, Baptist, United Brethren, Congregational, the Friends, Unitarian, Episcopal, Reformed, Catholic, Evangelical and such minor groups as Disciple, Mennonite, Dunkard, Free Thinkers and Winebrenarian.

Soon, Burrowes issued more detailed religious instructions. Each day there was to be a morning and evening worship in the large study hall consisting of the reading of Scripture, the singing of hymns and prayer. Grace was said before all meals. A circular was sent to the local ministry inviting them to come and give Sunday sermons. If a church was nearby, the children could go there for the Sunday service. Immediately after breakfast on Sunday, the children put on their best Sunday dress. Then there was an exchange of library books. At ten o'clock the orphans assembled in the large study hall for Sunday School. The large church service, if they did not go to a neighboring church, was held in the afternoon. Sunday night saw a hymn sing. [23]

A diary kept by one of the principals shows how the officials of the schools took these religious mandates seriously:

"Thurs, Jan 5, 1882: Revs Rigor and Roads, Methodists, delivered their illustrated sermon to the school. Over 179 professed Christ. Ministers took names of boys and girls.

Tue, Jan 10: Children's prayer meeting.

Wed, Jan 25: Children's prayer meeting. Clyde Brown in charge.

Model of the Harford School Chapel

Sun, Feb 19: Frank Murphy spoke in Sunday School.

Wed, March 29: Prayer meeting both in the chapel and class room." [24]

A visitor to the Chester Springs School said it was his "good pleasure to visit the Chester Springs School last Sunday. The children were taken by their teachers to a near church where seats were appropriated for them and prayers by the congregation were offered for their proper training and spiritual conversion. In the evening, the Principal conducted them in religious exercises, the children singing and uniting orally in the Lord's Prayer. During the afternoon, we noticed one of the boys earnestly reading a library book. We questioned him as to his future prospects. We discovered that although he was but fourteen years of age, he had lately joined the Methodist Church and that he intended devoting himself to the ministry of Christ. This one instance proves the blessing the schools are destined to be to future generations for the service of God." [25]

Harford School Girls Exercising

Probably not too many of the orphans were really concerned about Christian morality and where their soul was destined to go.

Certainly most of the children were more worried about such prosaic problems as: 'What am I going to get to wear?' 'What am I going to get to eat?' 'When can I play?' 'What kind of 'wuppin' am I going to get for hiding my baseball bat under the front porch?' [26]

Younger Boys, Chester Springs School

As to clothing, each of the boys wore a facsimile of the uniform of their deceased father - a blue jacket with 'gilt eagle buttons,' grey trousers, a kepi style cap and black shoes. The boys got three of these outfits each year. They were fitted and sewn by a local tailor. Each school received a $25.00 clothing allowance for each orphan. The prices of these items seem reasonable enough: fifty cents for the jacket and thirty cents for the trousers. All the rest of the clothing of the pupils - boys' undergarments, shirts and socks - and everything for the girls - dresses, undergarments, hats- were sewn up by the older girls in the so-called "sewing room" on the numerous sewing machines under the direction of a female adult seamstress. At one school the girls constructed in one year: "104 blue Henrietta dresses, 56 brown serge dress-

SOS girls used Singer sewing machines

es, 47 school dresses, 216 gingham dresses, 73 white dresses, 487 drawers, and 134 fancy aprons."[27]

The boys wore their uniforms every day and were allowed to wear them on vacation at home. Both sexes had heavier coats for winter wear. Clothes-hooks in each of the dormitories enabled the children to hang their clothes when not in use.

SOS Boys in Uniform

After breakfast each morning, the orphans were inspected. Woe to the child who was missing a button or had failed to shine his shoes. He lost his play privilege for the day.

The only concern for the principals was how quickly the orphans, particularly the boys, wore out their clothing. The uniform of a boy was pretty much threadbare at the end of the year. So, it was simply passed on to a younger boy.

Certainly, the orphans were better clothed than children in the average rural home where most children went barefoot in summer.

The food they ate, however, was about what they would have gotten at home. As Superintendent Burrowes stated in 1865,

Suetta Marley and inmate John Wilhelm wearing 'typical clothing' of the SOS

"wholesome, sufficient food is all that is needed in childhood. Rich dishes and dainties are prejudicial." [28] However, his suggested breakfast of "butter, milk, boiled eggs, boiled potatoes, and a warm meat preparation" was a little more elaborate then what the children actually received. [29] Most of the schools served a breakfast of coffee, molasses, and mush (cornmeal). This is why the orphans liked to see Mrs. Hutter, the female inspector, appear – 'Here comes Mrs. Hutter, she will bring some butter.'

The main meal was at noon. It was usually a soup (bean or potato) with a little meat or perhaps a meat pie with vegetables and dumplings, usually more dumplings than vegetables, and the ever present molasses, bread and coffee. Supper was about like breakfast - bread, molasses and coffee.

The meals were eaten in silence with the boys and the girls sitting at separate tables. Their adult supervisors ate with them. Everything was done at the tapping of a small bell - at the bell everyone stood for grace, another bell and they all sat down. At

Meal at 18th Century Orphanage

the last bell, after thirty minutes of nourishment, all filed out of the dining room.

With all this regimentation, one can understand why the children prized their free time. They could play outside in decent weather after breakfast, at the fifteen minute morning recess, after the noon meal, and after the afternoon recess. Each of the sexes had their own playground, a grassy area, usually in front of the school. Popular sports for the boys were shooting marbles, Copenhagen, pass and catch a corner, hunt the skipper' and baseball. Some of the schools had their own ball teams which

Scotland School Croquet Club, 1907. Scotland, PA.

played neighboring institutions. At Chester Springs, it was called 'The Alerts.' "On Saturday afternoon, the Alerts played the Mutuals of West Pikeland and won, 4 to 3." [30] For the girls, jumping rope and hoops along with croquet were popular.

In the evening, the orphans were allowed, under adult supervision, to go to the library or the music room. The library at Chester Springs had 1200 books and 16 periodicals. The music room consisted of five pianos and two organs. Most of the schools had a brass band. The one at Chester Springs consisted of thirteen pieces and was conducted by a teacher from Philadelphia. The local paper said it compared "favorably in efficiency and deportment with more professional organizations. [31]

But so called "games of chance" were a 'no, no.' One mother inquired of Superintendent Burrowes if the playing of dominoes was permitted. He replied that it was neither approved or practiced in any of the schools and was "wholly prohibited. Even when not playing for money, the habit of appealing to chance is pernicious. Youth should be taught to depend on their own efforts. The habit of acquiring anything without labor especially when de-

Brass Band Chester Springs School

termined by chance, is gambling. And this habit leads to adult gambling and therefore is to be avoided as demoralizing." [32]

Some of the schools organized literary societies which greatly pleased the state officials. Inspectress Attick in 1888 was impressed with the one at Chester Springs: "I think it would be advantageous if similar societies were organized in all the schools. The exercises which consist of addresses, declamations, readings, debates and music are interesting and much enjoyed by the children. The evening is spent not only very pleasantly but profitably, and thus are beneficial to all." According to the principal of Chester Springs, all the officers of the society were orphans who learned how to conduct the meetings. But there was always a teacher present. [33]

However, even with all these so-called "necessities," the orphans were still reminded of the need to lead a well disciplined and orderly existence. If the child did not learn to lead a well disciplined and ordered life, there was always the stick across the seat of the pants. "Our discipline has been strict," claimed one principal. [34]

Jumonsville boys posed with Frederick William Gritton head of the State orphanage at Jumonsville, P.A.: one boy is playing the violin, Jim Payne, the driver is in background (1867)

While all of the authorities protested the use of corporal punishment, most of the principals freely admitted that they made frequent use of the pine paddle. After all, many of these orphans were "mean and vicious, malicious and devilish. They pulled hair, fought and even knocked down teachers." [35]

Sometimes "in terrorem" was the only way to teach these future citizens respect for obedience and authority. [36] According to one principal, his success as a disciplinarian was his greatest accomplishment as an educator:

"The want of the age is the spirit and letter of obedience, not only in society and the state, but in all departments of life. Hence, if this want is not met, there is insubordination and failures in business and society. We have tried to train our children to obviate these difficulties."

He then told of how a recent graduate of the school had returned to thank him for teaching this supreme fact of life:

"I was a bad boy at school and hard to manage and I owe all of my success to your restraints and instruction."

This, noted the principal, was a "great comfort to a disciplinarian." [37]

Punishment of the orphans for most of the officials was an absolute necessity. "For lying, stealing, swearing, and kindred faults, we must have severe penalties," said the principal of Chester Springs. "I believe that corporal punishment is the surest cure." [38]

But of course, such a testimonial was hind sight. It is doubtful if most of the orphans appreciated corporal punishment. Those children who lived near a city often rebelled against the school system and fled the institution. The local paper for the Chester Springs School which was only 40 miles from Philadelphia, said that two boys, aged thirteen and fourteen, "escaped yesterday at 3:00. They were found at the residence of the younger one's

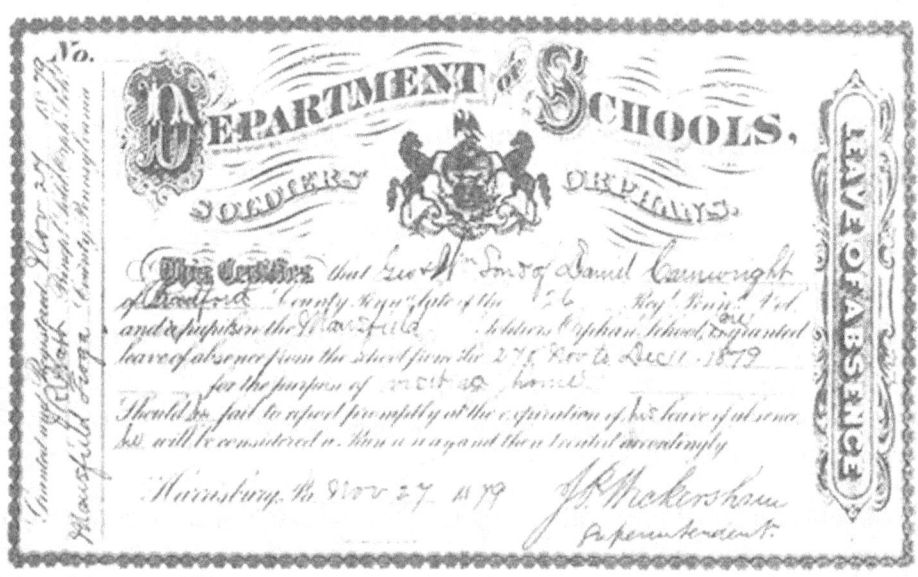

Leave of Absence pass, 1879

mother in Reading and complained of harsh treatment, having walked all the way over there, 30 miles. . .Both will be returned to the Springs." [39]

Only a week earlier a boy tarried too long from his vacation in Phoenixville and "Officer Kelly was notified to arrest him and send him back. [40]

Similarly, "George Dersch, aged 15, ran away, but was sent back to the school." [41]

And on "Monday, two of the boys at Chester Springs ran away to Phoenixville . . . After their disappearance was discovered, they were followed and found at their homes, one in Gordonville and the other at Marietta. When they left the institution they asked a brakeman to take them to the Lancaster county line, which the trainman did. The lads then boarded a freight train and went to their homes. They said they were dissatisfied with the schools. Constable Smith took them back to Chester Springs." [42] In fact, a

SOS Boys Fire Drill

boy in 1876 was accused of setting fire to one of the buildings at Chester Springs, during which he and four of his friends escaped to Pottstown "last Tuesday evening. They were sent back to the school on the following day." [43]

But, perhaps, the grievances of the orphans were not as serious as the *bete noir* of the state officials and the proprietors. Their major worry was the health of the children - protecting their charges from disease. The nineteenth century was still the age of epidemics. The orphans lived in a close environment. The dormitory rooms were small and the children usually slept two to a bed. Sanitary facilities were primitive. One had to go outside to a privy to relieve himself. Night stools, which had to be emptied in the morning, were universally in use. They bathed once a week - on Saturday. It was more like the so-called 'old fashioned sponge bath' where a bucket of water was poured over the child

Typical "Night Stools" used at the schools

and he just 'soaped down.' More than one state inspector criticized such a practice, suggesting more adult supervision at the

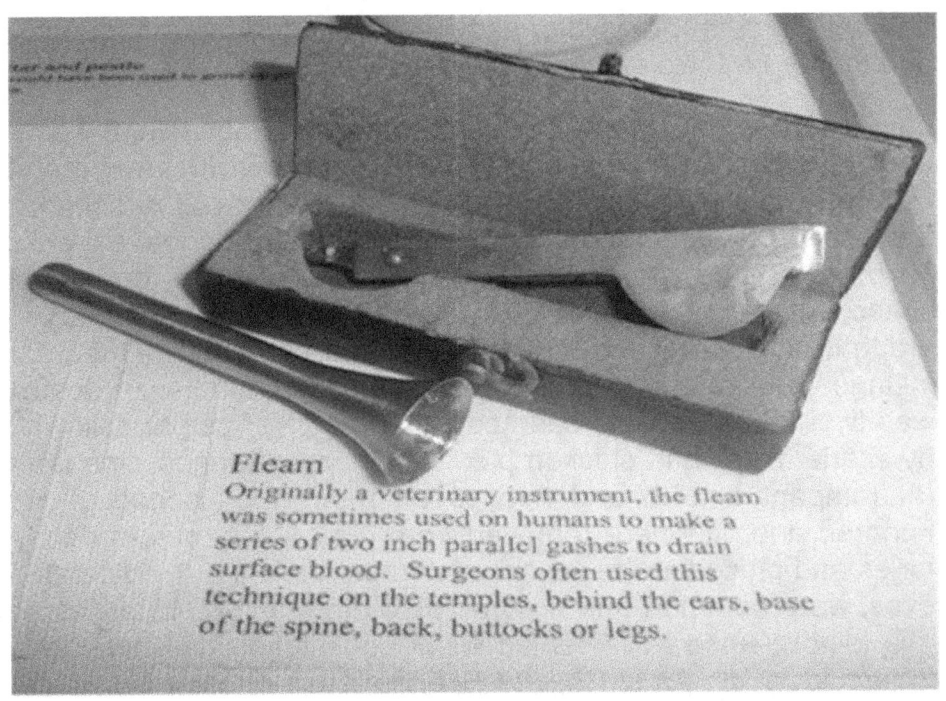

Chester Springs School Infirmary Fleam

Chester Springs School Infirmary, 2015

bathing room, that the water should be changed more frequently, and that more towels be made available.

Thus, if a contagious illness hit any of the schools, it was a time of real concern for the authorities. In practically every report by a principal over the twenty five year history of the schools, the local official first recounted any major scourge or gave thanks for being spared any deaths. In a later study of the ten largest schools, it was discovered that between 1865 and 1893, the average mortality rate was four and one-half percent. In 1882, for instance, out of a total of 2,500 orphans, the number of deaths was twelve. [44] Measles seemed to be the chief culprit, followed by scarlet fever and chicken pox. At Chester Springs, "measles ran rampant" in 1887 and thirty-seven of the whole school of one hundred and fifty were removed from their two separate dormitories and placed in the school's infirmary building. [45] 'Ulcerated eyes' were common and children also died of such illnesses as "hip joint disease . . .inherited weak constitution and hereditary tuberculosis." [46] As at Chester Springs, each of the schools had a small separate infirmary building staffed by a resident nurse. A local doctor was always on call. Dental care was not routinely given even though a few of the schools had dental service.

Sometimes an episode would take place to break the monotony. At Chester Springs in 1873 the local GAR gave the school a really big American flag measuring eight hundred square feet. The problem was that it needed a long flag pole. A former sailor, now the chief engineer of the local iron works, agreed to climb up the two hundred foot pole and attach the flag. Unfortunately a rope snapped and he fell to the ground and supposedly remained unconscious for four days. The local paper followed the whole episode with some suspense. The former sailor recovered his consciousness but lost the use of one arm. Subsequently, he entered a law suit against the doctor of the school. He asked for $20,000 in damages. Finally, the court adjudicated the matter. And the doctor won. The flag, incidentally, was later raised on a pole half the length of the original one but as the paper claimed "can now be seen at a long distance." [47]

Because of the unchanging routine and the threat of disease, it was welcome news when the orphans were told that they were going to take a trip outside the school. The most famous excursion was the one of March, 1865. Superintendent Burrowes was worried about the legislature appropriating funds for the upkeep of the newly formed system of orphans schools. So, with the aid of the Pennsylvania Railroad and Tom Scott, its president, 345

SOS Parade

orphans were brought to Harrisburg to "wow" the legislators. They marched from the railway station in the state capitol to the capitol building, the boys resplendent in their new "dark blue gold-laced caps, blue roundabouts, and grey pantaloons." And the girls in "brown hoods, black cloth capes and checked frocks. Each of the three schools was proceeded by its drum and fife corps."

Needless to say, the orphans were loudly cheered by the spectators along the route. Burrowes spoke first to the legislature. He said that it "had been noised around that these children were starving and kept filthy without proper clothing, to which he directed the attention of the audience and asked if what they saw made such reports true. He then called on the children for songs, recitations, and other exercises . . .Master Henry Albert of the McAlisterville School made the opening speech (thanking the governor for his efforts). . . His delivery was fine, and his words were greeted with applause. The girls of Mt. Joy sang 'Dear Old Flag' . . . Master David Leach from [the] Paradise [School] delivered an original address which he spoke with real eloquence. He thanked the people of Harrisburg for their [kind reception]. The boys of Paradise sang 'Uncle Sam is Rich Enough to Send All of Us to School' to the great amusement of the audience. Master George Jacobs of the McAlisterville School recited the 'Orphan's Appeal,' an original poem. The Mount Joy [School] girls then sang 'Tenting On The Old Camp Ground." Master Stevens, son of a dec'd Pennsylvania Reserve soldier recited 'Our Father' [saying that if in the need arose, the orphans would rally around the flag like their fathers] The McAlisterville School sang 'On! On! On! a sequel to 'Tramp! Tramp! Tramp.' This was greeted with great enthusiasm. Maurice Fitrey of the Paradise School from Harrisburg

Dress Parade Chester Springs School

delivered an oration on 'Our Heroes.' His reference to Abm. Lincoln was loudly cheered. The valedictory was delivered by Master William Hunter, son of a former member of the 1st P.[ennsylvania] V.[olunteers] He promised that the boys would improve, tendering thanks to Superintendent Burrowes and the teachers. The exercises closed with the children singing the 'Orphan's Prayer' which brought tears to many not used to weeping." [48]

So successful was the March 1865 trip, Burrowes decided to take ten of the schools to Philadelphia on July 4, 1866 when the Pennsylvania Civil War battle flags were to be returned to Independence Hall. This was quite an undertaking with almost 700 orphans joining the adult participants in a great parade to the Hall. The logistics of the trip were staggering: "The food on the way will consist of bread, cheese, and cold meat. A significant number of drinking cups should be taken. No sweet cakes or confectionary is allowed. The teachers, principal, matron and male assistant are to have the pupils under constant supervision. No pupil is allowed to leave ranks . . . Not a single act of improper conduct has been heard. The Superintendent has received numerous expressions of admiration on the deportment of the children." [49] Falling in behind Governor Curtin in the parade, "the girls rode in ambulances escorted by fully dressed firemen and delighted the spectators with singing patriotic songs. The boys, wearing their military uniforms marched alongside the 'war-torn' veterans and their tattered flags. Whereas earlier in the day the streets of the city had swarmed with raucous young boys setting off fireworks and generally running amok," this was a noteworthy contrast as noted from the preceding description of the ten schools penned by a correspondent of the Philadelphia Inquirer. [50]

And there was always the local Fourth of July parade. In 1876, the pupils of Mt. Joy participated, with the boys in their "beautiful blue uniforms and thirty six girls seated on a large wagon trimmed with flags wearing white dresses representing the thirty-six states and a "very beautiful young girl in the center [of the wagon] dressed as the 'Goddess of Liberty.' All drawn by six horses." [51]

Sometimes an individual school would go quite a distance to give a performance. In 1882, the Mt Joy School went over one

Spring and the Nymphs of the Woods, Chester Springs School

hundred miles by rail to Danville, PA. On the evening of Monday, May 29, the 133 orphans rehearsed in the Danville Opera House. The next day they went to the neighboring town of Catawissa to parade and then returned to Danville where they gave their show in the evening in the Opera House. The contingent started home the next day at 12:30 and got back to Mt. Joy at 5:30. They traveled in three special railroad cars. The principal described the journey as a "grand success." [52]

But the highlight of each year for both the pupils and their mentors was the annual examination and graduation that took place in early summer when the school closed temporarily and the orphans went home on vacation. This was a public event and hundreds of adults would attend - newspaper editors, doctors, ministers, mothers of the orphans, GAR members and often even the governor of the state. The examination was completely oral. There were no written questions. The adults of the era appreciated oral declamation. The examination was more entertainment than a test. Usually, an official from the state bureaucracy was in charge.

At Chester Springs in 1886, the Deputy State Superintendent of Schools asked "Who is the President of the United States? 'General Grant,' responded a half-dozen voices. Then a hearty laugh followed as the better posted ones sang out, 'Governor Cleveland.' One little girl wrote 'fryed' on the blackboard and she looked bashed when a little fellow in blue stepped forward and wrote it correctly." [53] Probably the graduating sixteen year olds were asked more difficult questions such as 'Give the nine rules for the use of capital letters? Name the fundamental rules of arithmetic? Describe the three most prominent battles of the late Rebellion?' Of course, the children had been prepped ahead of time by their teachers on what to expect. So, this was simply the common educational practice of memorization and recitation. Sometimes the exam turned humorous. One official asked a "question to which no answer was given. The examiner expressed himself well that none of the pupils knew how much James G. Blaine's plurality had been in the county in the last election. He hoped that they would never find out since he would like to forget it himself." [54]

Another pupil showed a great knowledge of Lancaster county where the Mt. Joy School was located. The questioner had no prize for the boy. "Reaching into his pocket, Mr. Henzel unhooked his Waterbury watch and gave it young Fowler, remarking, "This watch keeps all kinds of time; if it gets out of gear, any blacksmith can fix it." [55]

But the highlight of the day for everyone who attended including the children was the noon meal. It was a dinner that probably the children only enjoyed once a year. At Chester Springs in 1886 it included roast lamb, potatoes, lima beans, stewed tomatoes, salad, coleslaw, coffee, tea, pie, cake and preserved peaches. [56]

After this feast, the boys demonstrated their proficiency as soldiers by doing their military drills. Then the girls performed

Girls of Chester Springs School, Examination Day

Tressler SOS Home

their calisthenics. At one examination, one adult visitor claimed that the girls "did especially well, and while the boys did well, the girls surpassed them in calisthenics and other exercises." [57]

At the end of the day, the orphans bade their adult visitors goodbye. At Chester Springs, they gave the departed three cheers and a tiger. [58]

The last major problem that those who ran the schools faced was how to fulfill the work requirements of the orphans. Nothing was allowed to interfere with their intellectual and moral training. But still the children had to do some kind of physical labor. The girls were rather successfully occupied in household duties like cleaning and the sewing of their garments. But it was another matter for the boys. In the summer, they could work in the garden and the fields with the resident farmer. Usually the school was able to raise enough food for their own use: potatoes, corn and beans. This taught the boy how to use a hoe at least. Some of the schools even kept pigs and cows. Chester Springs had the largest farm of the system. There were six acres of potatoes, one and a half acres of beets, two acres of corn, six of wheat, four of oats, one of grapes and one-half acre of cucumbers besides four thousand cabbage plants, one thousand celery plants and three thousand onions. By August 6, twenty bushels of strings beans had been harvested. The stock embraced three horses, three cows and twenty hogs. [59]

But what could the boys do all year around? The answer was some sort of industrial education. But, as Inspector Cornforth realized as early as 1874, this created a big problem: "To furnish instruction and facilities for such practical skills would involve an

Shoe maker apprentices

outlay of funds which the temporary nature of the schools do not warrant." [60]

Thus, before 1889, few attempts were made to establish industrial training. Some of the schools put in a shoe making shop or a blacksmith shop. But these only trained a few pupils. Most of the schools simply had the orphans making brooms.

These attempts underscored the weakness of industrial education within the system. It was too expensive to set up a comprehensive industrial program.

6
SCANDAL

Through it all, those in charge of the Soldiers' Orphan Schools of Pennsylvania succeeded in arguing the merits of the system. For over twenty years, the schools were described as one of the most successful and popular philanthropic undertakings in the history of the Commonwealth.

Educators, historians, journalists, legislators - all commented favorably on the schools. Teachers in a convention in 1867 resolved to express their gratification towards the benevolent enterprise.[1] The author of a popular state history at the time noted the advantages accruing to the whole community: "A body of well-instructed and morally trained young men and women will be given to the Commonwealth." [2]

Remarks made in the legislature when the life of the schools was extended invariably dwelt upon the positive contributions. In 1878, a lawmaker claimed that no other state sponsored system had given so much satisfaction to the people of the state. [3]

Three years later another legislator told his colleagues that the soldiers' orphans were "fast becoming the most useful citizens of the state."[4]

Frank Leslie's Illustrated Newspaper, A "Vicious" girl enters a similar program and after being fully reformed graduates displaying good manners

In 1883, the horrors that the system had spared the state were described to the state assembly:

"Why if only one, if only a half dozen of these children would be cast out and become vagabonds and useless to society and addicted perhaps to vice and crime, it would be enough of an impulse to continue the schools" [5]

"Criminal" children brought in for questioning

The state's newspapers vied with each other in extolling the virtues of the system. Every spring correspondents from the local press attended the end of the year examinations. They came away convinced that the young scholars were the equal to any in the common school system of the state. The examinations were always a grand success since the orphans usually answered the questions correctly. [6]

The military drill on the parade ground exhibited the moral and physical training necessary for the "battle of life." Most of all, the journalists were impressed with the order and discipline that permeated these institutions. Good behavior was the mark of a well-run school:

"We are more convinced than ever that the military discipline as shown at White Hall [Soldiers' Orphan School] is the best method of managing schools as it teaches the boys and girls obedience, promptness, order, system and every other quality from which come live men and women." [7]

SOS Boys on Horseback

All of this approbation was not lost on those who operated the system. They noted with satisfaction these numerous and friendly observations. [8]

Why then, with all this favorable opinion, did the Soldiers' Orphan Schools of Pennsylvania come to such a sudden end in 1889? How did this popular institution of the latter nineteenth century become a historical curiosity by the early twentieth century?

February 22, 1886 marked the beginning of the end of the Soldiers' Orphan Schools of Pennsylvania. On that date, the tabloid Philadelphia Record headlined the storm that was about to break over the heads of the soldiers' orphans:

"SOLDIERS' ORPHANS

A SYNDICATE'S TRAFFIC UPON HUMANITY

Official Corruption, Neglect, Discrimination

Bathing Orphans In Pickle Barrels

A Furnace Cellar For A Playroom

Crowded Three and Four Children Into One Bed

Forcing Them To Wear the Same Clothing

In Winter and In Summer"

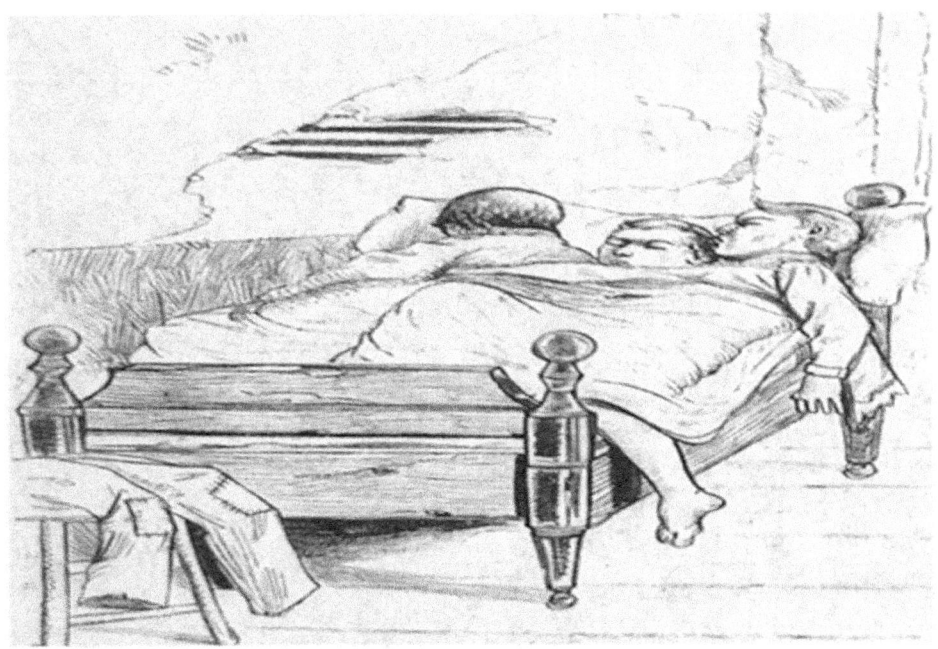

SOS "Three sleep in a bed"

The rest of the article, which took up nearly all of the front page, described how the once "grand purpose" of Pennsylvania was being "prostituted" for the sake of human greed and callous neglect. The "children of the state" received little schooling since they were forced to spend most of their time "scrubbing floors and peeling potatoes." Sleeping quarters were foul smelling, poorly ventilated garrets. Profits as high as fifty thousand dollars a year were being rolled in by the private owners as they fed their charges for as little as three cents a meal.

John Norris, the author of the tragedy claimed it was the infamous Dotheboys Hall come to life. Like Squire Squeers of Dickens' fictional English boarding school, the proprietors of the Soldiers' Orphan Schools in their lust for money had turned the state's pride into "pestholes." [9]

The P.A SOS compared to Dickens Squire Squeers

The reaction to this revelation was instantaneous. There were words of outrage on the front pages of practically every daily newspaper in the state. The schools were a "State's disgrace," a "humiliating Revelation." The perpetrators of these crimes must be brought to justice. Imprisonment was not good enough for them. The present system of state aid had to be changed and most of the private schools, if not all of them, should be closed. [10]

Just as vehement was the indignation of the thirty-five thousand members of the state Grand Army of the Republic. This veterans' organization, while it had never had any official connection with the system, had always taken an active interest in the institutions and had come to feel that it had a special duty to protect the welfare of the children of their fallen comrades.

Practically all of the four hundred posts of the state GAR passed resolutions condemning the alleged outrages. [11] On February 24, 1886 only two days after the original Record exposure, the state commander of the GAR. announced that he was setting up a five man committee to investigate the schools. [12] "The Grand Army Marches Against the Plunderers of the Orphans," heralded one newspaper. "When The Conspirators Learn of the Veterans' Movement Their Hearts Will Seek Their Boots." [13]

Except for an informal questioning of the state officials of the schools, however, the GAR. committee never undertook an inquiry of the schools. Instead, the official state investigation of the system was conducted by the governor of the state, Robert E. Pattison and his attorney-general, Lewis Cassidy. Accompanied by Norris, the Philadelphia reporter, the three visited ten of the schools between March 5 and March 26, 1886. The state's top two elected officials questioned over one hundred witnesses and took seven hundred pages of testimony. This tour was reported in detail in the state's newspapers. The national press published descriptions of this official probe. [14] The influential national weekly, Frank Leslie's Illustrated Newspaper, printed "graphic" pictures showing what the Governor had found at one of the schools. On April 15, 1886, the results of the gubernatorial probe were made public:

Frank Leslie's Illustrated Newspaper. A SOS "Neglected Patient"

"The facts proved by the testimony unhappily establishes the substantial truth of the Philadelphia Record's charges. The testimony shows a most pitiful, cruel and inhuman neglect of the children as well as suggestions of depravity and immoral practices that are too vile for enumeration. The entire system shows human greed, speculation and heartless bargaining." [15]

SOS 'Play Room in the Cellar"

Governor Pattison, although he fired the two inspectors of the central state superintendent's office and requested the resignation of the state super-intendant of the Soldiers' Orphan Schools, claimed that he could do nothing about the conduct of the private schools since they were the creation and responsibility of the state legislature. Like most political law making bodies, however, it took the legislature a long time to grind out the inevitable conclusion to the whole sordid affair. The fate of the Soldiers' Orphan Schools of Pennsylvania was not decided until March, 1889.

Gradually, the controversy disappeared from the pages of the state's press but the issue was kept alive by the annual encampments of the GAR. In 1887, a GAR. committee suggested the cessation of state payments to the schools until the proprietors were cleared of all of the governor's charges.[16] The following year, a similar committee of the veteran's organization said that the best solution to the whole unfortunate situation would be the establishment of one central school under the direct control of the state.[17] Finally at the February encampment of 1889, the members of the Army were informed by the state commander that a delegation from the GAR. had been meeting with a legislative committee for the purpose of revising the system which had existed since 1864.[18] In March 1889, the Pennsylvania General Assembly by a unanimous vote approved these deliberations. The law changed the original one of Governor Curtin and Superintendent Burrowes.

The original state superintendency which had administered the system for twenty-five years was abolished and replaced by an eleven man Commission made up of the governor, five legislators and five GAR. men to run the schools. Furthermore, the formerly privately owned schools were turned into public schools. The Commission would rent the facilities, purchase all of the supplies and hire and fire the principals, teachers, and attendants.[19] This provision, however, proved to be only temporary. In July, 1889, the Commission closed five of the schools and transferred the orphans to the remaining six schools. This action was hailed by the state's press as being "too good to be true."[20] By 1892, three more of the institutions were closed. The real intent of the state's political leaders was revealed in 1893 when the legislature authorized the building of a single establishment to educate the soldiers' orphans. This was the Industrial School for Soldiers' Orphans built at Scotland in the central part of the state. By 1912, the last of the orphans of the old system were transferred to this new and wholly owned and operated public institution.

In brief, this is how the Soldiers' Orphan Schools of Pennsylvania (1864-1889) came to an end. It was a story of scandal,

charge and counter charge. But there was more to the culmination of the system than the expose of a Philadelphia journalist, the cries of disbelief and horror by the state's citizenry, the wounded pride of the G.A.R., and the determination of an embarrassed governor and legislature to make amends for a serious situation. Three social and economic forces, characteristic of late nineteenth century America, conspired to weaken the original plan of Curtin, Burrowes, and Wickersham.

7
Industrialization and the End of the System

First, Pennsylvania and the nation in the last fifty years of the nineteenth century underwent a powerful economic transformation. The Industrial Revolution came to the North American republic. Formerly it had been mainly an agriculture nation. By 1900, the United States was one of the dominant industrial nations of the world. And Pennsylvania was deeply involved in this change. By 1870, farming, formerly the chief economic enterprise, was fast losing out to the rising tide of manufacturing. An impressive and new industrial complex was based on the Keystone State's rich mineral resources of iron, steel, coal and oil which was tied together by an impressive railway network.

The implications of this industrial transformation upon the youth of the state were enormous. Pennsylvanians, like most Americans, had always demanded that a common school system pay some practical dividends tied to the economic concerns of life. Now, what had formerly satisfied a largely farm population, no longer seemed to fulfill the needs of a modern, industrialized society.

One group that had to face this new problem were those officials in charge of the Soldiers' Orphan Schools of Pennsylvania. Their reaction to this revolution explains, in part, why their enterprise came to an end.

Like most of the state's children, the soldiers' orphans came from the bottom classes of society. Very few of them, it was claimed, would ever aspire to become professionals or achieve a more superior social status. "These children," said the first superintendent of the system, "are not to be trained up under the impression that they are exempt from the necessities of labor for their bread." [1]

The problem was that the qualifications needed before 1864 were no longer sufficient for industrial specialization. "I can obtain plenty of laborers," Superintendent Wickersham quoted a Philadelphia manufacturer, "to do the common kinds of labor about the factory, but I cannot obtain a sufficient number of skilled workmen." [2]

Cannery Working Immigrant Families, late 1800's

Simply putting some tools in the hands of a 'jack of all trades,' or a "a mechanical mechanic," no longer guaranteed a job. The times called for intelligent and skillful workers. [3] "What we need," claimed Superintendent Wickersham, "are schools where the boys can be trained in the sciences of industry."[4]

This need for job preparation was closely tied to the influx of foreign workers. The officials of the Soldiers' Orphan Schools claimed that thousands of trained industrial workers were arriving from the long time industrial nations of Europe. "Few American boys," said the female inspector of the orphan schools, "learn a trade. We are obliged to send to Europe for our trained workers while our own workmen are compelled to occupy lower positions at lower wages." Mrs. Hutter admonished the proprietors of the private schools to "wake up" to the need for industrial education.

Ellis Island late 1800's

Puck April 28.1880 by Keppler

Hutter was also worried about the political menace of these foreigners. They had radical beliefs that were a threat to America, "a nation of freemen." [5]

The corollary to this professed danger of foreign radicalism was the fear of the domestic left. Like most spokesmen of the upper classes in America, these officials of Pennsylvania were highly critical of organized labor. As a protest movement against the status quo, the banding together of workers suggested anarchism and socialism. In her report of 1879, Mrs. Hutter congratulated the "bravery and decision" of the governor for using the National Guard to quell the Great Railroad Strike of 1877. While this threat to the public order had been silenced, the female inspector was sure the "railroad troubles" had certainly showed the people what communism means." [6] According to Mrs. Hutter and her colleagues, one of the reasons that the workers were turning to the dangerous unions was their inability to find jobs. As unskilled rejects they needed the new skills of the industrial age. "The workers strike," said Superintendent Wickersham, "when they see

Great Railroad Strike, The Burning of Union Station 1877, Pittsburg

no other way to remedy their wrongs." [7] The officials in charge of the soldiers' orphans always came to the conclusion about the problem of providing their charges with the needed skills of the new industrial age:

"This complaint [said Wickersham] is a universal one. The people will before long manifest their wishes in this matter in such a way that those in authority will find it unsafe to resist them." [8]

In an attempt to meet the challenge of industrialism, the officers of the orphan schools first turned to what one called the "regular manner" of getting a job skill, the apprentice system. [9] Outlined in the original plan of 1864 and made official in the law of 1867, the superintendent of the system was given the authority to bind out an orphan to a master craftsman where the child would learn a useful trade. [10] However, those in charge of the soldiers' orphans soon realized that too much faith had been placed in this traditional method of job training. It was difficult to persuade employers to take on even the "best and brightest boys" as apprentices. It was "too expensive and arduous" for the factory owners. [11] Moreover, the claimed restrictive policies of the unions plus the arrival of skilled immigrants shut the soldiers' orphans as apprentices out of the labor market. It was almost impossible to enforce the old punitive provisions of the apprentice system. It was difficult to compel boys to serve out a long apprenticeship. According to Superintendent McFarland, "They tire of restraint quite too easily and abscond to avoid restraint and punishment." [12]

Thus, the indentured method of teaching job skills was never used in the soldiers' orphans system. The orphans were never bound out. [13]

With the admission that apprenticing was a dead letter, those in charge of the enterprise turned to the only alternative - instruc-

Child Workers replacing bobbins on machinery, late 1800's

tion in industrial skills inside the schools themselves. In fact the same 1867 law that mandated the apprentice system also charged the proprietors of the schools to "provide the greatest variety of mechanical employment." [14] During the life of the system, every school had some form of industrial training.

At one, the wards were "fitted to make a living" by learning how to construct wooden cabinets. At another, "the industrial system was tested with good results," as the boys learned how to make bricks in a recently built kiln.[15] The Titusville Herald suggested that the local Dayton school was doing its job as the pupils learned the printing and shoemaking trades. [16]

Apprentice and Printer - late 1800's

Although there were claims of success, it is evident that these attempts at industrial education were no more successful than the old apprentice system. Inspector Columbus Cornforth, in particular, was critical of the method of setting up small shops in the schools. One or two shops making brooms or shoes scarcely met the challenge of the new era. Further, he doubted if the orphans were really learning very much. There was a "fearful propensity to tinker to become masters of nothing." [17]

Superintendent Wickersham seconded this criticism. In 1871, he told the private school principals, "MERE JOB OR CHORE WORK DOES NOT FURNISH THE ACQUIRED INDUSTRIAL DISCIPLINE." [18]

Even the local press was unsure about the job training the orphans were receiving. "I was greatly pleased," said one reporter after a visit to one of the schools, "with one exception, namely the boys should receive instructions in skilled labor."[19]

Finally the principals of the schools recognized the total inadequacy of their job training. One confessed that the making of shoes and brooms was not diversified enough and did not enjoy a great degree of success. Two years later he admitted that these trades were no longer pursued. [20] Another said that quite a few of his charges had a flair for "mechanics" but the opportunities were not available to teach them the new industrial skills. [21] As the principal of the Mt. Joy School summed it up: "It is a matter of regret that it has not been within the power of the management to provide the diversity of labor which is desirable." [22]

Three factors worked against the development of a bona fide industrial training program in the Soldiers' Orphan Schools' system. First, the attitudes of the educators who ran the system reflected the prevailing debate over the respective merits of traditional, intellectual and cultural studies versus those that were supposedly more practical. The allegiance of the schoolmen of the Soldiers' Orphan Schools was clearly with the former. They were academicians of the old school who held that a useful education was that of the mind (reading, writing, arithmetic, algebra, geometry, logic, and grammar) and that the teaching of physical trades subverted the primary goal of a basic education.

The first superintendent, Thomas Burrowes, claimed that to learn how to do physical labor was as much a part of a child's education as the study of algebra. But, he claimed that the one was subordinate to the other. Burrowes ridiculed the demands of the adult workers for "bread and butter sciences." They were ignorant to denounce the truly "practical" subjects -"the classics and languages." [23]

For the orphans, Burrowes in his "General Rules" stated the official philosophy on the mixing of intellectual and manual studies:

"Inasmuch in this complicated process there is a starting point of instruction to which all the others must be subsidiary, and inasmuch as the custom and wisdom of our ancestors have decided the instruction of the 'MIND' [italics mine] to be that starting point . . . The regular education of these orphans in the school room is hereby recognized and declared to be that department which is to have precedence . . . This rule is without exception." [24]

This admonition did become the rule for twenty-five years as all of the schools followed a daily routine of six hours in the classroom and two hours at work.

Even as late as the 1880's and the demand for industrial education, those who ran the schools were still arguing the primacy of the traditional studies. The children arrived at the schools with little prior schooling. Their time, therefore, had to be taken up with the vital common studies. Industrial training was impractical and it would be "positively harmful" to the future welfare of these "children of the State." [25]

Closely tied to this stand on the supremacy of intellectual studies was the belief that it did not really matter if a student failed to understand what he was doing as long as he succeeded in the performance of the task. His attitude was all important. This aim of the educators in charge of the orphans was essentially non-cognitive. The development of character was more important than either intellectual or manual skills. Time and again the words "discipline" and "self- discipline" appear in the rhetoric of these officials. The chief task of a teacher was to inculcate the correct norms and attitudes to preserve an orderly society.

This ideal carried over into the opinions of the officials on industrial training. The chief goal of all industrial education, said Superintendent Wickersham in 1877 was to "form habits of industry and create a taste for work." [26] The key outcome was the development of character, "the discipline," as one principal put it, "in the habits of punctuality, promptitude, and attention as in his school room work." [27]

The essential failure of industrial education was not that the orphans did not work. They worked, probably more than the two hours allotted each day. The problem was that their work was not giving them the skills necessary for a future job in the new industrial society. As a soldiers' orphan testified in 1889, "While I was there, I learned how to make brooms. When I went home to Philadelphia, of course, there was no use for my service at all, so I drifted into some other state and finally came back and started in another business entirely." [28]

All the orphans did chores around the schools. The boys chopped wood and carried coal ashes. The girls made the beds and swept the floors.

The officials of the schools, however, were not worried about the absence of a meaningful industrial education. Skills in the technical operation of modern machines were unnecessary. What counted for job success was self-reliance, industry and perseverance or as Superintendent Wickersham called it "pluck." [29]

Inspector Cornforth might lament the lack of industrial training, but in the same breath, he stated "yet much is done in forming habits of industry and instilling correct views of labor." [30]

This academic lack of industry in the teaching of the new skills was closely related to a second factor that worked against meaningful industrial education in the Soldiers' Orphan Schools. They were rural institutions. Even though many of the orphans were from the city, they were all designated as "farm children."

"It is not intended," said the first superintendent, "that the children should be taught trades or sent forth prepared in the mechanical pursuits. Instead they are exercised in those pursuits to which their fathers would have provided them." [31] They were being prepared for their common station in life - as farmers.

Chesterfield Springs SOS girls working in the school field

Cost was a further issue that negated industrial training. The schools were generally far removed from the industrial centers of the state. They would have had to purchase their own modern equipment and hire qualified instructors. This, to the private owners was not cost effective. [32] The products produced in the school would be too expensive to sell. The children with only two hours each day for work would never be able to manufacture products which could compete on the open market. Against the "products of skilled labor," the products of the orphans would only be that of "unskilled apprentices, necessarily crude and unworkmanlike." [33]

Furthermore, the principals recognized the facts of automation. One proprietor in 1878 claimed that if he put more machines in the school, then proportionately fewer children could be trained. Consequently, he abandoned the idea of setting up industrial training and substituted a "farming program" instead. [34]

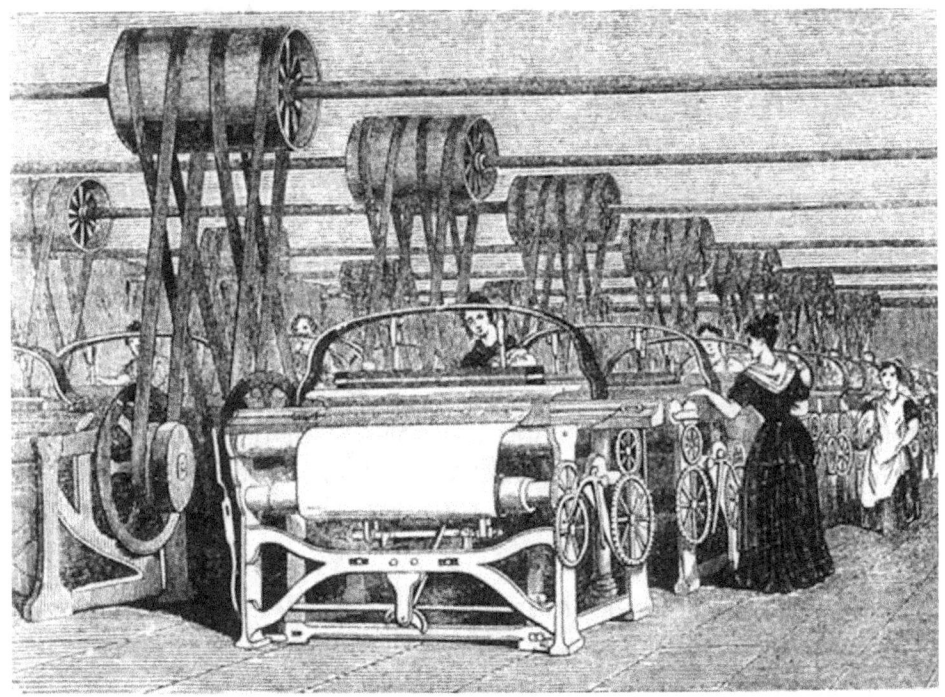

Automated Philadelphia Textile Factory, 1877

All of the officials, however, said they were willing to spend the funds for industrial education if the state would guarantee the permanency of the system. Five times the legislature had extended it. Would the state keep doing it?

The principals/proprietors argued that it was unreasonable to ask them to spend a great amount of money for machines if the schools were going to close in the near future. [35] This argument of permanency seemed particularly valid after the sensational revelations of the Philadelphia newspaper in 1886. It would cost, said one principal the next year, five thousand dollars to buy the equipment for a bona fide industrial education program. Since the schools were scheduled to close in 1890, this, he said, was too much money to spend for machinery that would soon be standing idle in a vacant school. [36] Even Superintendent Higbee in 1888 said it would be foolish to undertake this new industrial education:

"Still wilder, and more chimerical is the thought that on the threshold of closing the schools, these proprietors could in any way be induced to do it." [37]

Thus, to the educators, state and local, who operated the Soldiers' Orphan Schools of Pennsylvania, manual training was an impossible and confusing goal. Tradition and economics told them to go slow. They realized, however, that the demands of the new industrial age made such industrial training imperative. One inspector cited this deficiency in the education of the orphans. But, "how," he lamented, "shall it be supplied?" [38]

One solution could have been the establishment of one or more actual industrial training schools. But until the so-called Scandal of 1886 broke, there was little interest expressed by those in charge of the orphans for such a program wholly sponsored by the state.

The amazing developments of 1886 finally gave the industrial education program its real impetus. The sensational revelations of the Governor Pattison investigation seemed to reveal that the original 1867 law specifying special instruction in industrial science was clearly being broken. The principals admitted to Governor Pattison that neither industrial nor mechanical pursuits were taught. There were no shops or tools. The male attendants who were charged with this part of the orphan's education confessed that they had no "mechanical ability." [39] Worse yet to the governor was the passing off of chores as industrial education. "Yes sir," replied one proprietor to Governor Pattison, "the manual training of the boys is doing chores about the farm, paring apples and potatoes and baking, and helping in the washroom." Another principal said the "industrial department" was washing, scrubbing and chamber work. For the governor, all of this was "sheer hypocrisy." What was called industrial education was really the use of the orphans as "unpaid servants." [40]

While the executive investigating committee made no recommendations on how to alleviate this unfortunate situation, it soon became evident what would be the final result of these charges of industrial neglect.

The state superintendent of the Soldiers' Orphan Schools, E.E. Higbee, in a letter to Governor Pattison now claimed that he had misgivings about the existing program of job training:

"I am unwilling to take the whole responsibility of these schools as regards to their adoption of the work required. I had to take them as I found them."

The superintendent suggested that all the schools in the western part of the state be combined into an institution at the abandoned state hospital in Erie. For only seventy-five thousand dollars, this facility could be turned into a school for "full industrial training." [41]

Significantly, persons other than those identified with the orphans were destined to lead the final drive for a state owned and operated manual training school. James Beaver, the Republican successor to the Democrat Pattison as governor in 1887, was highly interested in industrial education. In his inaugural address, while he did not mention the soldiers' orphans, he did devote over two pages of his address for such a program in the common school system of the state. [42]

The next year he made the same suggestion for the orphans. At a conference of the principals of the state's normal schools discussing industrial training for the future teachers of the state, Beaver steered the subject to the soldiers' orphans claiming that it was not wise to continue the present method of job training. He suggested that special, model schools housing the orphans be set up at the normal schools. Here the children could receive both an academic and industrial education. But the proposal elicited no discussion from the assembled school men. A few months later Beaver made public his intentions. Since the existing system was due to close in 1890, perhaps now was the time to try something new for the soldiers' orphans so they could take "their legitimate place in practical everyday life." A separate industrial school seemed to be the best solution.

As a first step, the existing system in place since 1864 had to be abolished. And Beaver took the lead. The GAR. legislative committee that eventually wrote the bill ending the Soldiers' Orphan Schools, met with the governor in early 1889 and reported they had Beaver's support. [43]

Superintendent Higbee likewise reconciled himself to the intent of the governor. "I shall be fully satisfied," Higbee wrote in April, 1889 with "whatever he [Beaver] may do." [44]

James Beaver

Entrance to Soldiers' Orphans Industrial School, Scotland, PA

In 1892, final success came to those who had been agitating for the establishment of a single school owned and operated by the state government itself. The newly formed Soldiers' Orphans Commission which had replaced the superintendency sent such a proposal to each post of the GAR. Sixty-two of the sixty-three posts said "yes." [45] In December, 1892, the Commission recommended to the legislature that a manual training school for the soldiers' orphans be established at a central location in the state so that the children could be "taught the trades that will equip them to go into the world and maintain themselves." [46] Such a law was passed in May, 1883. The Scotland Industrial School for Soldiers' Orphans was established in Scotland, Pennsylvania about sixty miles southwest of Harrisburg. It received its first children in 1895. In time, the orphans from the original and remaining schools were transferred to this newly built facility, wholly owned and operated by the state government. The Scotland school undoubtedly surpassed the fondest dreams of those who had long advocated manual training. By 1904 it possessed printing, tailoring, and wood working departments. The students were being taught electricity, telegraph and typewriting. There was a machine shop and engine room.[47]

The new school seemingly had succeeded where its predecessors had failed. The tragedy of the original 1864 schools was that they had failed to meet the challenge of the new Industrial Age. Part of the problem was administrative. The schools were rural institutions and their private owners were lacking both the desire and the financial capability to provide industrial education. The rest of the trouble was an administrative failing. The educators who ran the initial program of aid to dependent children were too traditional in their thinking. Morality, not work skills was their aim. Believing in the primacy of academic studies, they failed to see the need for a truly useful, more socially adaptable type of education.

Thus, the demise of the Soldier's Orphans schools of Pennsylvania, 1864-1889 can be traced to their failure to provide an adequate industrial education for the orphans.

8

The Administrative Failure of the System

There were two other important reasons for why this system of charitable aid came to an end. One of these failings had to do with its organizational structure. A system of public relief that relied on private owners seemed to be at odds with the growing tendency in the latter nineteenth century for the state to take over total control of relief projects.

The system seemed to be a half and half arrangement. The state superintendency and its inspector team were supposed to regulate the schools. The actual schools, however, were privately owned. So, a number of problems ensued.

First, were the schools non-profit or profit making enterprises? Evidently the legislature of 1867 believed that the former was true. Along with the act legalizing the system, the lawmakers approved a measure that exempted the privately owned schools from local and state taxes. This was done on the assumption that the schools were charitable entities along with being part of a state system.[1] But the legislators were the only ones who followed this kind of logic. Almost everyone else connected with the schools considered them to be private and non-charitable. As such, they were free to make a profit.

The first superintendent early stated the case for capitalistic enterprise in explaining why most academy owners were unwilling to enroll soldiers' orphans. He noted that they thought little money could be made by running a school for orphans. They expressed a willingness to help the orphans but held back because of their concern for "pecuniary profits."[2] Another state official phrased it as "not a very great inducement from a worldly point of view to furnish every necessity [for each child] at $2.50 a week."[3]

Most of the state authorities saw nothing wrong with the private owners cutting down on expenses to increase profits. Few attendants had to be hired since the children were used as non-paid labor. Food raised by the boys found its way to the dinner table, reducing the proprietor's grocery bill. The establishment of the little shops that made brooms and shoes was rationalized in terms of possible sales to the general public.[4]

Girls making brooms, late 1800's

Furthermore, the profit-making propensity of the men who ran the schools should have been expected. The educators who owned the schools were hard-headed, practical and down-to-earth. Many of them engaged in other business enterprises. More than one was extolled as "a man of wealth, a true businessman." [5] Some were newspaper editors. Others operated stores and farms.

Rev. A.B. Waters, proprietor/principal of the Uniontown School, was a typical owner. Waters, a minister turned educator, besides seeing to the needs of 165 soldiers' orphans, preached to a local Lutheran congregation, was an assistant United States postmaster, operated a farm of 150 acres, ran a flour mill, and owned a clothing factory. [6]

While admittedly on a small scale, these proprietors of the Soldiers' Orphan Schools were examples of the hard working, energetic "Captains of Industry" so admired in the post-Civil War era.

It was one thing, however, to justify the making of profits by these proprietors, and something else that over the course of the life of the schools became a real problem. What, for instance, was a fair monetary return for a school owner? How much of the $150 paid them by the state should the owner to spend on the children? Most important of all, should the quest for monetary gain be the chief motive for operating an orphan's school? Did not each proprietor have a responsibility to consider the charitable welfare of their charges ahead of dollars and cents? Such questions as these came early to the attention of the state officials who were responsible for the oversight of the proprietors.

State Inspector John Cornforth often publicly questioned the humanitarian sincerity of the owners:

"These professional philanthropists, in order to hide their greed for gain, make loud and constant proclamations of their self-sacrificing love and yet possess not one drop of the genuine milk of human kindness." [7]

Superintendent Wickersham, usually a stanch defender of the private owners, seemed to be equally worried about their "extra exertions" to keep their schools full of their clients. In the late

1870's, he reported that rumors had reached him concerning the employment of paid agents by the proprietors to find eligible soldiers' orphans. While he had no proof of this practice, the Superintendent warned the local school boards who checked on those children eligible to receive state aid to scrutinize all applications for admission made in behalf of the soldiers' orphans. [8]

> forts on the occasion referred to.
>
> **Soldiers' Orphans.**
>
> The mothers or other relatives of destitute orphans of deceased Pennsylvania soldiers and sailors, who reside within the city limits, are requested to meet the Superintendent of the Soldiers' Orphans at the Union Benevolent Association on the 22d, 23d, 24th and 25th of the present month, between the hours of 9 A. M. and 4 P. M., to hear applications and make arrangements for the admission of said orphans into the schools and institutions provided for them by the State.

But except for these two negative reactions, no one officially connected with this state system of relief before 1886 ever questioned the financial motives and practices of those who actually were in charge of the Soldiers' Orphan Schools.

On at least two occasions, members of the State Legislature charged the owners with financial improprieties. In 1871, a state senator claimed that a soldiers' orphan was being cared for at a cost of ninety dollars a year even though the owner who was in charge of his welfare received $150.00 per child each year plus a twenty five dollar clothing allowance. "This," believed the lawmaker, "[was] an enormous profit for somebody." [9]

Four years later, another lawmaker questioned whether children of veterans who had not been killed in the war should be admitted to the schools since he believed the proposed legislative act was largely to further enrich the proprietors.[10]

A similar concern was expressed in 1883 by a newspaper editor in the state capitol. He was sure the owners of the schools were behind the movement to extend the life of their schools: "If the parties who profit have their way, the schools will never close! "[11] Likewise a committee of the Grand Army in 1881 was worried about the owners skimping on the welfare of the children simply to make more money. [12]

But these three statements were the only public criticisms of the alleged greed of the private owners. As a newspaper editor noted in 1886 after the so-called scandal broke and the ensuing investigation by Governor Pattison took place, all of these early attempts to expose the conditions of improper and undue gain evoked the counter-charge by the defenders of the owners of disloyalty to the memory of the orphans' fathers. It was a brave legislator or newspaperman who took issue with anything connected with this popular, patriotic enterprise.

It was not until the Pattison investigation of 1886 that the proprietors felt the sting of financial impropriety. One of the most sensational charges that came out of the Governor's inquiry was undue profiteering. Most of the state's press now were convinced that the schools were only being operated as a business enterprise. "Money making," said one editor, "seems to have been the chief aim of the management."[13]

And what profits! The Uniontown school owner supposedly made in one year what he had originally paid to purchase the property. At Dayton, the original investment of fifteen thousand dollars was now bringing in nine thousand dollars a year. One irate taxpayer informed the governor that this school was being run only in the interest of the stockholders and not for the care of children.

Some of these stockholders even supplied the school with provisions at a higher rate than that bid by other retailers. There was even the story that one owner had bragged he had made over forty thousand dollars in three years. Now he was in Europe, far from any possible legal proceedings.[14]

Details of how agents were employed to find orphans to keep the schools filled came to light. According to the Pattison report, the rivalry for profits by the owners was so intense that they paid the agents handsome fees to recruit soldiers' orphans. Through the agents, the proprietors, it was charged, offered glowing inducements to the mothers of the orphans. That principal of the Uniontown schools even admitted to the governor that he paid each agent five dollars for each of the fifteen orphans procured, while another owner said he paid a public school teacher a similar sum for four children. [15]

Perhaps the most interesting reference to the use of an agent was a fictional account appearing in a journal. In one episode of "Only A Soldiers' Friend", the author has the German principal of the fictional "Mt. Olivet School" (really the Mt. Joy School near Harrisburg) meet his agent in a local saloon:

"Vell, how many you got?"

"Two, a brother and a sister, replied the agent."

The author of this fiction then concluded that:

"The darkest day for the family of Jim Jones (the fictional name of the deceased veteran) was the day when the agent of Public Munificence entered their lives." [16]

Even worse than the use of agent was the charge by Governor Pattison that the owners were skimping on taking care of their charges in order to squeeze as much profit as possible out of the payments from the state.

When a child outgrew his uniform, it was simply passed on to an orphan smaller in size, threadbare or not, "so much in the manager's pocket." To save money the orphans were packed into small, stifling, and poorly ventilated dormitories. On a steady diet of cornmeal and molasses a child was kept alive at a cost of three cents per meal. [17]

FRAUD AND CORRUPTION

In the Soldiers' Orphan Schools of Pennsylvania.

PHILADELPHIA, PA., February 22.—The *Record* this morning publishes a six-column article on the management of the soldiers' orphan schools of Pennsylvania, which alleges not only official discrimination, neglect and corruption, but also that a syndicate is profiting at the rate of $50,000 a year in the management of four of the schools. A voluminous array of figures is given to support the allegations. In some of the syndicate schools children are packed together in bed-rooms and school-rooms like herrings. Fifty-three children were removed last fall from good schools, single beds and pleasant surroundings in the Northern Home, to sleep in foul rooms at Chester Springs. At Mercer, in consequence of the penurious methods employed by the management, some of the boys bathed in pickle barrels, two to each barrel. At Chester Springs some twenty-five or thirty pupils have been deprived of all schooling for three months. All regard for the children seems to have been subordinated to a heartless grab for profit, and this evil influence has been carried to such an extent that a premium of $20 a head has been paid to agents to recruit children for various schools. It is because of this competition and because of the comparative scarcity of orphans that the schools are now half filled with children whose parents are living off the $350,000 appropriated annually by the State to pay for feeding, clothing and educating these wards of the State. It is calculated that nearly $90,000 is absorbed in excessive profits.

SOS "Boys Making Bread"

With all these financial improprieties now out in the open, the public now agreed the days of these profiteers were numbered.

As one editor pronounced:

"The traffic in the necessities of little orphans will cause an uprising among the people of Pennsylvania that will end in the discomfiture of the men who put money in their purses while neglecting their duty."

And the Attorney General of the state was even more specific. As he cross examined the owners, he told them:

"Gentlemen if you will not provide for these children, you are going out of business." [18]

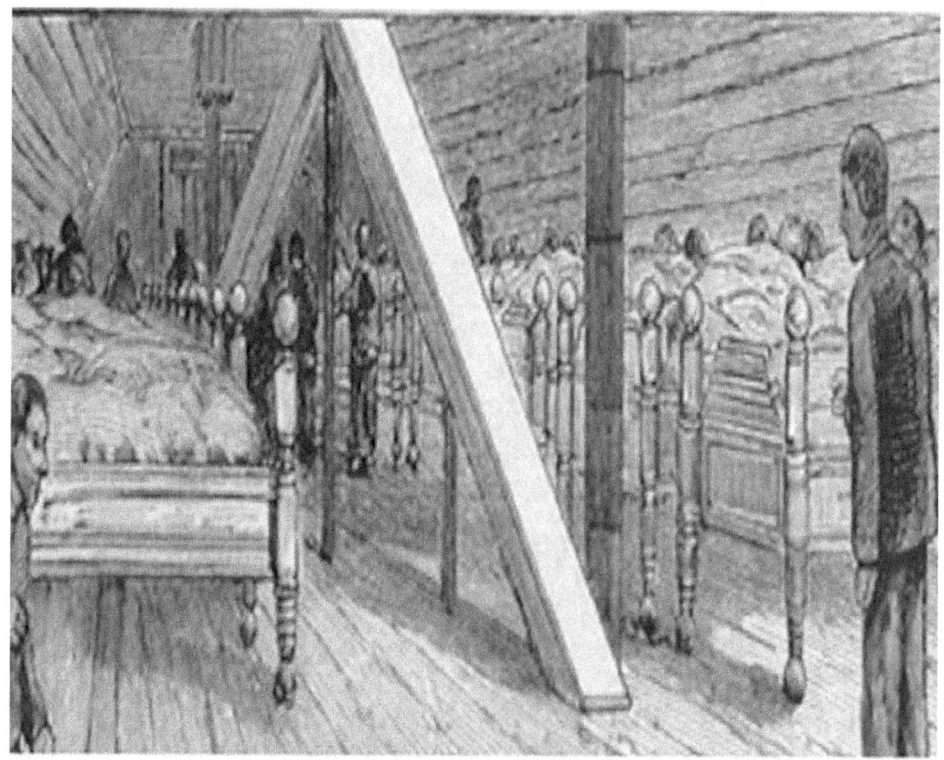

SOS "Attic Dormitory"

Even if these critics overstated their case, it was clear that the income of these private school entrepreneurs was much in excess of their expenditures. Later, when the state took over complete operation of the system, almost one hundred thousand dollars less was spent each year for the same service provided by the private owners. In 1889, the last year of the Soldiers' Orphan Schools of Pennsylvania established in 1864, the state paid out three hundred thousand dollars to the private owners. The next and first year of total government control, the expenses were reported to be less than two hundred thousand dollars. [19]

When it came to financial irregularities, four of the schools of the original plan seemed to be worse of all: Mercer, Mt. Joy, Chester Springs, and McAlisterville. What these four private institutions had in common was the nature of their ownership.

The abhorrence of late nineteenth century America towards economic combination is well known. Corporate businessmen were portrayed as brigands cheating and plundering to gain their vast wealth. The domination of a particular economic by a "Ring," "Trust" or "Syndicate" seemed to contradict the most basic of American virtues - individual competition and free enterprise. There seemed to be something sinister about a few men banding together at the expense of society.

It was no wonder that the Pattison revelation of a "Soldiers' Orphan Syndicate" aroused the anger and indignation of the people of Pennsylvania in 1886. A monopoly minded business arrangement was robbing the public treasury and making money off of starving children. The tone was set by a newspaper in western Pennsylvania:

"We read of coke syndicates, and oil syndicates and railroad syndicates, but we don't remember ever having heard of a soldiers' orphan school syndicate. It seems, however, that such a syndicate does exist. Its object is to speculate off of the noblest charity the state ever knew." [20]

The leader of the "Soldiers' Orphan Syndicate" was George F. Wright, a former state senator from Mercer county in the northwest part of the state. In 1874, Wright and three others purchased the Mercer Soldiers' Orphan School. According to their critics in 1886, the four were out for more schools. They aimed to control all of those that housed the most orphans. By 1885, they owned the four largest schools in the system. [21]

Wright and his fellow partners never served as school principals of their schools. They seldom visited the institutions and employed others to run the properties. Wright and his friends were the business managers of the schools A central purchasing office in Mercer bought and distributed supplies to the four schools. Unlike the individual owners who secured their supplies in small quantities from local merchants, the syndicate purchased in large amounts from wholesale dealers as far away as Cleveland and Philadelphia. [22]

George Wright

But the critics of Wright never really noted these legitimate techniques of decreasing costs. Instead, attention pointed to more disreputable practices. The syndicate really abused the use of agents. The other owners paid five dollars per child. Wright was accused of going as high as twenty dollars a head. [23] The syndicate went their individual competitors even better in skimping on the orphans. Most of the owners furnished at least fifteen towels in the washroom. At his Mercer school, Wright saved money by putting out only four. Feeding their charges at most of the schools for three cents a meal was bad enough. But getting by on a penny a meal was criminal. [24]

In January 1884, two years before the so-called scandal broke, Wright sent his manager at Mt. Joy coffee that was far better than that usually served the children. The employee was informed that there was soon going to be an encampment of the GAR at the nearby city of Lancaster. The principal was cautioned to expect the veterans to visit his school. But manager Hipple was not to throw out the old coffee. When the GAR visitors left, he was to resume using the regular beverage. [25]

Wright was characterized as a "sharp and shrewd businessman . . . parsimious and stingy." [26] The individual owners made money; Wright, "piles of money." [27] The final report of the Pattison investigation revealed that the annual profit of the syndicate on the four schools was seventy thousand dollars a year. Wright supposedly had made enough money to buy a hundred thousand dollars worth of property in his native county of Mercer.[28] To most Pennsylvanians, Wright and his fellows were the worst of the "Almighty Dollar Patriots." [29]

Practically everyone in the state from the governor to the local newspaper editor was convinced the syndicate had to go, that this system of corporate ownership had to be broken up. Even the head of the system, the Superintendent of the Soldiers' Orphan Schools was unsure of joint control. Superintendent Higbee had originally defended this kind of arrangement. In March, 1886, he stated that just because several schools were under the control of a syndicate, this was no reason to consider these owners worse than the individual proprietors. They were at least more economical. [30] But two months later, Higbee had second thoughts. Because of the machinations of Wright and friends, the whole system of schools was suffering:

"It is an unwise policy and has been from the beginning that there should be combined ownership of the schools. It is out of this single element in this situation that the present excitement and all of its misrepresentation and mischief could alone have arisen." [31]

SOS "Pickle Tub Used for Bathing"

Practically everyone in the state after 1886 believed that all of the private owners, corporate and individual, had gone beyond what were reasonable profits. For this kind of charitable business, the profits of the owners were too large and they were growing rich to rapidly. [32] Superintendent Higbee summed up this almost universal opinion:

"But whatever else may be certain, one thing is sure; the management of this patriotic charity should be of such character as naturally to preclude the thought of large profits. If the profits of any owner or manager have been so large as is claimed in certain quarters, it is a fraud upon the public faith and an outrage upon the generous instincts of our common humanity." [33]

At the same time, no one denied the owners their right to make money. It was too much to expect them to donate their property and services. "These proprietors would be marvels of perfection," said one editor, "if they refuse to accept what the State gives them for taking care of the orphans." [34] After all, this was a contract system and those who held the contracts had the perfect right to make something out of them. [35] Call it temptation or just good business sense, the opportunity to make money - a lot of money- was too strong to ignore. [36]

"ROBBING SOLDIERS' ORPHANS" Newspaper Reports

In the end, the real fault lay with the nature of this unique system of relief founded during the Civil War. The real mistake was made in 1864 when the care of the soldiers' orphans was given to private entrepreneurs. By 1886, many of the newspapers of the state professed to be surprised that such a situation had developed. A system of relief based upon contracts was sure to attract dishonest men. As Governor Pattison claimed, "A system which permits the farming out of children at a given price a head is radically wrong and necessarily productive of evil results." [37]

As the details of high profits and penny pinching came to light in 1886, many citizens asked how these faults had escaped detection for so long. Why was it necessary for the governor to traverse the state exposing these financial improprieties?

According to the original law of 1867, either the superintendent of the system or the two inspectors were to visit each school every three months, staying at least twenty-four hours. If an institution was found deficient in following the rules laid down by the state, the contract between the owner and the state was to be annulled a once. As a lesser punishment, the inspecting official could refuse to sign the pay vouchers from the state until the irregularities were corrected. [38]

Until 1886, no one had questioned the performance of the three state supervisors. They claimed that they always made thorough inspections and that they tolerated no deficiency or abuse. Their visits were always unannounced. [39] The state's press echoed their approval. Superintendent Wickersham was "thorough and frank," while Inspectress Hutter was a "very capable officer of long experience." [40] The lawmakers of the state said that these inspectors were constantly traveling about the state checking on the schools. They were "conscientious and hardworking stewards" who never allowed an owner to send in a bill unless his school was in an acceptable condition.[41]

The inspection reports of the state inspectors were almost always favorable towards their clients. They had great faith in the good intentions of the proprietors. Even in 1886 when the storm broke over the system, Inspector Sayers admitted that in his ten year tenure, his reports seldom found fault with the operation of the schools. His 1886 report for four of the schools, except for one entry of "tolerably good" for the clothing at the McAlisterville School were all in the category of "very good" or "good." Notable, three of the four schools tabulated were from the "syndicate." [42]

But at the very time when a state inspector was commending the private owners, most observers in the Commonwealth were convinced the operation of this state charity was a blot on the name of Pennsylvania. Less than three months after Sayer's evaluation, his replacement as Inspector, Louis Wagner, gave a far less complimentary picture of the same four schools, particularly the three syndicate properties. Now, there were eleven entries in the "tolerably good" category, three in the "middling," four in the "rather good," and one in the lowest rating, "very poor." "Very good" went down to three ratings by Wagner and "good" to seven. [43]

Allowing for exaggeration by the new inspector, it was evident that the schools were not in the flourishing condition described from their founding in 1867. In fact, as Governor Pattison made his way around the state, more than one proprietor admitted that the visits of the inspectors had been less than thorough. One teacher testified that the staff was informed two or three days in advance of the arrival of the inspector. Immediately, the school was prepared. Beds were fixed, new straw was put in the mattresses, and the whole school given a good scrubbing. A carriage was sent to the railroad station for the distinguished arrival and a special meal prepared in his honor. [44]

Nor did the inspectors always stay the required twenty-four hours. Most would arrive by the morning train and leave in the afternoon. According to one former pupil, the inspectors only had enough time to go once through the school, share a meal and "make a little speech to us to be good and we might be President of the United States."[45] There was also evidence that the inspectors failed to visit each school the specified four times a year. The principals claimed that three visits, sometimes only two, were not uncommon. [46]

Governor Pattison summed up these charges of neglect and incompetence. Even before Reverend Sayers and Mrs. Hutter arrived at the schools, they seemed to be "well disposed" to accept things in the best possible terms, "anxious to see merits and blind to all faults." "Their reports," continued the governor, " are of that general character and invariably present the schools in the most favorable light." He was convinced he would have found the institutions in a much better condition if the inspectors had "faithfully performed their duties." [47]

Most of the state's newspapers now came down hard on the male and female inspectors. All these years they had been "rattling around in a forest of eloquent but worthless rhetoric." It was "the Gospel of Gush, OILY GAMMON, A Great Eruption of Natural

Higbee

Gas, You Tickle Me and I'll Tickle You." [48] Even journals sympathetic to the plight of Sayers and Hutter had doubts about their performance. It seemed a case of state inspectors who did not inspect. [49]

Probably the most astute evaluation came from one the principals. He felt sorry for the two inspectors. No one should charge them with being insincere about the welfare of the orphans. If the two had any failing, it was their inability to perform their tasks:

"We feel that their mistakes, if any, were of the head and not of the heart." [50]

Ultimately, however, most of the charges against the state's bureaucracy were directed at Superintendent Higbee. Both the commissions and omissions of the two inspectors and the frauds of the owners were his responsibility. A highly respected and scholarly educator and theologian, Higbee suffered through a period of intense criticism after 1886. The governor and the press were almost unanimous in their condemnation of the Superintendent.

Like the inspectors, he was also accused of not making enough inspection tours and remaining the required twenty-four hours. Much was made of an episode that occurred in his office in Harrisburg. When informed of the alleged neglect of the children, Higbee supposedly turned on his heel, exclaiming contemptuously, "I guess they get more than they would have received at home." He was described as unsympathetic and a "bungler." "Right under his nose," the system was being highly mismanaged. "No man," said one journal, " is more responsible." [51]

However, many of the state's press felt sorry for Higbee. He had not done anything intentionally wrong. Instead as a Christian gentleman, the superintendent had believed in the best and doubted the worst of his fellow man. This was not a safe assumption when dealing with the hard headed proprietors. He did not realize that they were shrewd and calculating businessmen. He had simply been the wrong man for this particular position of Superintendent:

"He is not of that skeptical and aggressive nature which doubts all testimony and which pushes the principals and matrons to do their duty. Dr. Higbee was not selected with the view to such duties as these. These are perhaps hardly to be looked for in a professional educator." [52]

Higbee, himself, admitted to this essential failing. He had always believed that the schools were run by "humane managers

. . supervised by conscientious inspectors. Others have been entrusted, perhaps in too large a degree. Their reports we have accepted as being from honest men and women."

But the most serious charges were leveled at the official who kept the books in Harrisburg. His, said the governor, was a matter of "official discrimination and corruption."

Col. James L Paul, the chief clerk, audited the accounts and assigned the soldiers' orphans to each school.

According to Governor Pattison, Paul had used his official position to favor the "Syndicate" at the expense of the other owners. He saw, claimed the gubernatorial investigators, that the syndicate schools were always full. The non-syndicate Mansfield School was practically empty. The syndicate's Mercer property while able to house 275 children, held nearly 350 orphans. [53]

And even more startling to Governor Pattison was the fact that Chief Clerk Paul was a member of the "Syndicate." The head of the Syndicate, ex-senator Wright, enabled Paul to purchase (at a cheap price) a part ownership in both the syndicate's Chester Springs School and the one at Mt. Joy. It was now understandable, said Paul's detractors, why these two institutions had increased their enrollment after Paul secured this lucrative deal. Further, the official responsible for auditing the books of the schools was approving payments to himself.

To hide his involvement, Paul had his profits charged up as loans. The principal of the Mt. Joy school testified that he had written the word 'loan' over the dividend payment to Paul. But this headmaster could not remember why he had done so. When questioned, the principal said he did not think it would look good for the Chief Clerk if he appeared to be the owner of the school. The same explanation was given for the absence of Paul's name on the letterhead of the school. [54]

Digging deeper, the critics also found that the female inspector, Mrs. Hutter, also owned stock in the syndicate's Chester Springs School - five hundred dollars worth. Evidently she had never made any profit on it and she sold it at a loss in 1881. Still, the investigators in 1886 questioned the propriety of a state offi-

cial holding ownership, however small, in an institution she was supposed to be regulating in the public interest. [55]

As the administrative deficiencies of the schools unfolded in the spring of 1886, most Pennsylvanians were convinced that changes had to be made in the system set up during the Civil War.[56] Even if the charges against the owners and department officials were exaggerated, enough truth remained to show that there was something seriously wrong with this almost twenty-five year welfare service:

"The fundamental error of the Soldiers' Orphan Schools idea is that the management is entrusted to private hands without the state exercising over them efficient and constant oversight." [57]

Sayers

There had to be reform. Practically all of the state's press called for the resignation of Superintendent Higbee and Inspectors Sayers and Hutter. Some believed that the schools and particularly those of the syndicate should be put under new management. The most common suggestion was that all twelve of the schools whether "good, bad or indifferent," syndicate or non-syndicate, should be abolished entirely. "They have become the prey of lobbyists and corrupt officials." exclaimed one angry editor, "and it is high time that they come to an end." [58]

A few newspapers believed that state aid for the soldiers' orphans, in any form, should come to an end. The original patriotic purpose of helping the children whose fathers had died in the Civil War had obviously been served. Those orphans were now adults who had to make their own way in the world.[59]

The first official action was taken by Governor Pattison. On April 15, 1886 following his month long investigation, he demanded the resignation of Superintendent Higbee. Higbee, however, refused to resign. He claimed he had been confirmed by the state senate and only that body could remove him. Pattison was more successful with the two inspectors who were his direct appointees. Sayers and Hutter were fired on April 15, 1886.[60]

But this was all that was done. The private schools and the central state department continued to operate as in the past. After the initial revelations of early 1886, the so-called "Scandal of the Soldiers' Orphan Schools" disappeared from the pages of the press and from the thoughts of most people in the Commonwealth.

At the same time, it was evident that a persistent – if quiet – movement was underway to change the system set up during the Civil War. Principally, it was a matter of time. Under the law passed in 1885, the schools were due to close in 1890. Those identified with the schools knew that with all the unfavorable publicity of the spring of 1886, it would be difficult to extend the charity past 1890. As evidence of the unpopularity of the schools, in 1887 for the first time in over twenty years there was strong opposition in the state's legislature to the appropriation of funds for the schools. [61] Even Superintendent Higbee believed that now was the time to legislate a new method to care for the soldiers' orphans. [62]

Most of this impetus for change came from the Grand Army of the Republic. The GAR was anxious that the state continue to aid the orphans past 1890. In 1887, the Army showed their displeasure with the existing system by proposing that the funds be cut off to those owners who were guilty of neglect and fraud. The following year, the GAR went on record for the establishment of an industrial training program for the orphans. [63]

STATE CAPITOL, HARRISHBURG

Finally on February 23, 1889, the state senate at the behest of the GAR established a seven man committee which along with a similar delegation from the Army was ordered to "take into consideration all matters pertaining to the Soldiers' Orphan Schools." [64] This joint body held meetings in Harrisburg and Philadelphia. Most witnesses, as the committee members themselves, believed that the four syndicate schools should be closed. According to the chairman of the committee, there was not a lawmaker who could be reelected if he advocated continuing the schools of the "Syndicate." One witness suggested closing all the schools and placing the orphans out as foster children in the homes of the Grand Army men, the state paying for their board and education. [65]

A group of former students recommended that the state lease the facilities from the private owners and employ its own principal, teachers and attendants. The GAR members of the joint committee proposed that a twelve man commission including the governor, five legislators, five GAR members and the head of the state's public school system replace the Superintendency as the administrative arm of the state but that the contract system continue to be used except for the four syndicate schools. [66]

The bill that was finally reported out by the committee to the legislature contained certain features of the last two proposals. A state owned and operated system of relief for the orphans was now about to become law. An eleven man Commission of the Soldiers' Orphans minus the state superintendent of public instruction would administer the leased schools. The contract system was abolished. The former private owners now worked directly for the state.

The proposed law was non-controversial and passed both houses with little debate and a unanimous vote. The only amendment mandated that no former syndicate school could be leased as a state school. [67]

What happened next was anti-climatic. On July 15, 1889, it was reported that the new Commission had closed the four syndicate schools and the Mansfield School:

"The great deed has been consumated" …"This action is heartily approved everywhere."…"The people, backed by the press, have given the Syndicate a brain clout." [68]

One editor, however, believed this action of the Commission did not go far enough. All of the former private owners, now state employees, should be brought to justice for their neglect and profiteering: "The whole system of the Soldiers' Orphan Schools was wrong, founded on the wrong principle and continued for private speculation. The only way to cure the dog is to cut off his ears. ABOLISH ALL." [69]

The newspaper man soon got his wish. By 1893, three more schools were closed. With the building of the state industrial school at Scotland in 1893, the remaining schools were gradually phased out of existence.

CHILDREN'S HOME, YORK

Much of the failure of the Soldiers' Orphan Schools of Pennsylvania can be attributed to the state officials who administered the system. They neglected to institute industrial education. They failed to supervise adequately the private school owners. Seemingly, more could have been done to solve the twin problems of job training and state regulation. A different problem, however, constituted a third reason for the end of the schools. In this instance, circumstances were beyond the control of those who ran the system. Events external to and having nothing to really do with the care of the soldiers' orphans hastened the closing of the institutions. The Soldiers' Orphan Schools also failed because they became involved with the politics of the state.

9
Politics and the End of the System

Pennsylvania politics after the Civil War differed little from the rest of the nation. Pennsylvania was a Republican state. Between 1864 and 1889, with one exception, a Republican was governor of the state. The GOP also controlled the state legislature. But, the dominance of the Republicans was always in jeopardy. They never polled more than fifty-two percent of the vote. Pennsylvania earned a reputation as a "doubtful state." [1]

In truth, there was little difference between the state's Republicans and Democrats on the important issues like the tariff, currency, and regulation of syndicates. What really decided elections were the personality and appeal of the candidates. The aim was to retain party control and get into office.

Despite a lack of political substance, politics were constantly in the public eye. The mass circulation of partisan newspapers and the popularity of political rallies made politics a great avocation for Pennsylvanians - a pastime which they took with a vicious seriousness. Even a charitable enterprise like the Soldiers' Orphan Schools did not escape its pervading influence.

Inspector John Greer

All of the members of the state bureaucracy in charge of the orphan schools were political appointees. In an era of limited state government, the $1,500 to $2,500 per year posts in the Department of the Soldiers' Orphans provided lucrative patronage. All of the appointees were loyal Republicans. Chief Clerk Paul admitted that he owed his appointment to the Republican boss of his home county. [2] His successor was the nephew of the GOP leader in Franklin County. [3] Inspector Sayers had been chaplain of the Republican dominated state senate. [4] Inspector John Greer was a former Republican state senator. [5]

Factionalism inside the Republican ranks frequently led to disagreements over the filling of positions in the state soldiers' orphans bureaucracy. In 1867, Thomas Burrowes was not reappointed to the post of Superintendent of the schools by the new governor, John Geary. Burrowes was a political supporter of Geary's predecessor, Andrew Gregg Curtin. The new Governor was a "creature" of Simon Cameron, the acknowledged chief of the state's Republicans. [6] In the later nineteenth century, Cameron and Curtin contested for control of the GOP in Pennsylvania.

Likewise, in 1881 Superintendent Wickersham lost his position as head of the central state agency because he incurred the wrath of the regular Cameron machine. Three years earlier he had allowed himself to be put forward as a candidate for governor by the liberal, Curtin wing of the GOP. Needless to say, he lost the nomination. The victor and a regular party man, Henry Hoyt, gained his revenge in 1881 when he failed to reappoint Wickersham as Superintendent of the Soldiers' Orphans Schools. [7]

A similar political struggle at the local level led directly to the closing of one of the Soldiers' Orphan Schools. In 1872, the struggle between the Curtin, liberal Republicans and the Cameron, regular party men intensified. In Huntington County, the owner of the Cassville School, A.L. Guss, allowed himself to be put forward as a candidate for Congress by the Liberal wing of the party. Guss, who also owned a newspaper, became the leader of the dissidents. A bitter struggle now broke out between the two factions. Guss's opponents accused him of being "a monster and a fiend" in connection with his operation of the Cassville School. He was charged with "vilely assailing" thirteen and fourteen year

Governor John Geary

Henry Hoyt

old orphan girls, "luring them to the hills and groves." [8] Guss claimed that it was character assassination and that his foes did not have the courage to face him in a court of law.

A.L. Guss

But the damage had been done. The Grand Army of the Republic, an ally of the Cameron regulars, called for a legislative investigation of proprietor Guss and his Cassville School. On strictly partisan grounds, the legislative recommended that the Cassville Soldiers' Orphan School be closed and the orphans transferred to other schools. [9] The local Democratic newspaper while gleeful with the strife tearing the opposition apart, understood the more serious consequences:

"Thus endeth the great struggle of the waring factions now renting the Radical Party of this county . . .It was a bitter struggle in which the welfare of the Soldiers' Orphans was but a secondary consideration . . .We deeply and sincerely regret that the school is going to be removed. We are sorry that the Soldiers' Orphans find themselves between the upper and neither millstones of partisan hate . . ." [10]

These examples of how the schools became involved in politics are minor when compared with the events of 1886 and the so-called "Scandal of the Soldiers' Orphans."

As already noted, the leader of those who accused the officials of the schools of corruption and malfeasance was Governor Robert E. Pattison. Pattison was the only Democratic governor of Pennsylvania between the Civil War and the New Deal years of the 1930's. He had gotten his start in politics as city comptroller of Philadelphia and was regarded as being highly moral, scrupulously honest and reform minded. [11]

He became the Democratic candidate for governor in 1882. Hailed as a youthful and energetic crusader against machine politics and corruption, Pattison won the general election for governor narrowly defeating the regular Republican candidate. [12]

The political future of the vigorous, thirty-two year old Pattison looked bright. If he could make an imposing record for himself as governor, he might advance on the national political stage as a senator or even president. The only difficulty was that the career of Pattison did not advance according to plan. His program of civil service reform failed to advance in the Republican controlled legislature. He angered many Democrats by reappointing a Republican, E.E. Higbee, as Superintendent of the Soldiers' Orphan Schools. Pattison needed an issue to restore his luster as a reformer. The storm that broke over the soldiers' orphans in 1886 seemed to be the answer for the embattled, young and aggressive politician.

At least this was how the Republicans saw the investigation that Governor Pattison launched against those who administered the system of soldiers' orphans relief. The whole so called "Sol-

Robert E. Pattison

diers' Orphan Schools Scandal" was a "fraud " designed to further the political fortunes of Pattison and the Democrats. The Democratic governor was simply seeking "to manufacture political thunder." [13]

The alleged "stench" of the schools would never have entered the nostrils of Governor Pattison, "if Superintendent Higbee were not an eyesore in the eyes of anxious Democratic aspirants for the position as head of the Soldiers' Orphan Schools." The "Scandal" was simply a scheme to get the Republican Higbee out and replace him with a Democrat. [14] Pattison's chosen Democratic successor as governor, Attorney General Lew Cassidy, would participate in the investigation and gain momentum for his race for governor. Both Pattison and Cassidy would be hailed by the citizens of the Commonwealth as the saviors of the orphans. [15]

Lewis Cochran Cassidy

Of course, the modern historical interpretation of the "Scandal" has to take into account both Republican and Democratic political motives. Pattison of course denied that he was conducting his investigation because of politics. At the same time, however, a case can seemingly be made for the partisan implications of the Pattison investigation of the schools in the spring of 1886.

Six days before the governor announced his intention to make a personal investigative tour of the Soldiers' Orphan Schools, he received a letter from a political friend in Mercer county, home of the head of the "Syndicate." "As a citizen and a democrat [sic]," the correspondent had some advice for his leader. Pattison would be pleased to know that his administration was "generally" endorsed by both Democrats and "intelligent Republicans [sic]." It is the general opinion of both parties that a great outrage is being perpetrated."

To make himself popular, the governor was urged to undertake a thorough investigation of "Wright and Co." [16]

Later, as Pattison conducted his on the spot visits to the schools, he received more encouragement. One "uncompromising Democrat" told the governor to bring "the Republican rascals to justice." Another claimed there were many citizens of the state who were "delighted" with his efforts against the Republican owners of he schools. [17]

Democratic newspapers in the state saw a chance to embarrass the opposition. The Democratic paper that broke the alleged "Scandal," the Philadelphia Record, was sure that "political pressures" had perverted the original good intent of the state charity. The schools existed simply for the enrichment of a few Republicans "whose faces are well known in the lobby of the State Capitol." [18] Other journals echoed this political theme. Persons of political influence were taking advantage of the children. The chief organ of the Pattison governorship, The Harrisburg Daily Patriot, claimed that a "vast political ring" was reaping a bonanza large enough to enrich half of the "loyal statesmen of the Commonwealth." [19]

Three prominent Republican politicians were identified with the alleged infamies and frauds. Syndicate owner, George Wright, a former Republican state senator and GOP boss of Mercer County, more than any other legislator had pressed for the continuation of the system of orphan schools. In 1879, by a vote of 29 to 3, the senate had mandated the closing of the schools in 1885. One of the 3 who had voted no, and by implication for an indefinite extension, was Senator Wright. Wright was using his political power and friendships, said the Democrats, to keep his lucrative business enterprise in operation. [20]

A second prominent Republican to feel the force of this Democratic attack was George Pearson, chief clerk of the state senate and secretary of the Republican state executive committee. As the details of the syndicate's financial manipulations unfolded, Pearson was reported to be "very greatly agitated." [21] Apparently the young politician owned a quarter interest in the Chester Spring's Soldiers' Orphan School and had recently borrowed

Thomas Cooper

$1,000 from proprietor Wright without putting up any security.[22] A Republican newspaper even noted that "evidently Pearson wishes he had never had anything to do with a Soldiers' Orphan School." It headlined, "Pearson To Take A Back Seat." After a conference with the state party chairman, the erstwhile secretary decided to resign his post, "lest his interest in the schools be used to the party's detriment in the next campaign." "The party," said the Republican state chairman, could "not be compromised by one man's private relations." [23]

The third leading Republican reputation tarnished by the "Soldiers' Orphans Scandal" was state senator Thomas Cooper, chairman of the party's executive committee and the leader who said the party secretary, George Pearson, had to go into retirement. Democrats made much of the fact that while the orphans were being starved and ill-clothed, Cooper, Pearson and Wright were on a pleasure trip to California aboard Cooper's private railroad car which supposedly had been elaborately furnished from the ill-gotten gains of the "Syndicate." Cooper, as head of the Senate Educational Committee, had been largely responsible for the extension of the schools. He, Wright and Pearson had seen that the Grand Army of the Republic posts of the state signed and sent to the state legislature remonstrances urging the continuation of the schools. Thus, Cooper had swayed the vote of the lawmakers, prevented the end of the system, charged the Democrats and enabled the Republican "Syndicate" to become richer and richer. [24]

The Democrats did not stop with these attacks on the Republican state leaders. They also charged the Republicans who worked in the central agency that administered the Soldiers' Orphan Schools with fraud and inefficiency. Chief Clerk, Colonel James Paul, the Democrats claimed, did not have to be encouraged to keep the syndicate's schools full of orphans. Paul was a regular Republican Party man. Similarly, it was reasonable to expect Inspector Sayers to make favorable reports about the syndicate schools. He, too, was a stalwart Republican. [25]

Even Superintendent Higbee did not escape the insinuations of political partisanship. In early 1884, Governor Pattison had requested his Republican head of the schools to replace Chief Clerk Paul. Higbee held out against the entreaties of the governor until December 1885 when he dismissed Colonel Paul. But Higbee continued to insult the civil service tendencies of the governor. Higbee appointed Joseph Pomeroy, nephew of the Republican boss of Franklin County to the vacant post. Certainly Governor Pattison cried the Democrats had every right to demand the resignation of the partisan Republican, Higbee. [26]

All in all, the state's electorate were encouraged to believe that the Republican Party was responsible for the "Scandal of 1886." The Grand Old Party was identified with those who had conspired to defraud the state of thousands of dollars and who had neglected the welfare of the soldiers' orphans. The Democrats were sure these charges would aid them in the coming gubernatorial election. [27] "The Soldiers' Orphan infamies are properly charged to the Republican Party" summarized one Democratic journal. [28]

And the Republicans were worried. "I regard the whole affair," said Matt Quay, heir apparent to Simon Cameron as boss of the entire state GOP, "as unfortunate at the present time. It is very essential that the party should remain unified if we are to succeed in the fall." [29]

In their anxiety, the Republican leaders and press were as quick as the Democrats to castigate those Republicans tainted with the odor of scandal. "Hunt the rascals down," Simon Cameron was quoted as saying, "expose them." [30] "Senator Wright is now in the city but refuses to talk," reported the Republican Daily of the state's capital. "Let him step down and answer the charges or admit he has cohorted with thieves and perjurers." [31] Likewise, the Superintendent of the Soldiers' Orphan Schools, E.E. Higbee, a Republican, was urged by the party press to "RESIGN NOW." [32]

Soon, however, the GOP changed their tactics. The Republicans stood to gain little by agreeing with the charges of the Democracy. Somehow the odium of scandal had to be transferred to the opposition. Democrats, not Republicans, should be the ones charged with wrongdoing. The Republicans attempted to discredit the Democratic paper which originally broke the "Scandal." The public was reminded that the Philadelphia Record was a muckraking sheet. The sensational charges of its reporter, John Norris, should never be allowed to tarnish the reputation of the helpless children, let alone their aggrieved mentors. No one, said the Republicans, should create a sensation at the expense of the state's most honored charity. [33]

More than one Republican editor questioned the motive behind the article of February 22, 1886 in the Philadelphia paper. Governor Pattison supposedly quoted excerpts from the piece

Simon Cameron

before it hit the newsstands. Later, the governor's Superintendent of the Soldiers' Orphans claimed that Pattison was behind the original expose. The governor had chosen Norris for the "appointed work of defamation." Norris had spent several weeks in January, 1886 in the Superintendent's office in Harrisburg gathering material for his scurrilous article. At the time, Superintendent Higbee said, the reporter had let slip that he was acting under "high authority." [34]

Successful in casting doubts on the veracity of the Democrats' charges, the Republicans next turned their attention to the month long investigative tour of the Democratic governor. Pattison and his Democratic inquisitors were accused of greatly exaggerating, even falsifying, the true condition of the schools. The word was "ex parte." Pattison, it was charged, long before he started his personal investigation had made up his mind about the guilt of the owners. This premeditated assault was accomplished but stressed only one side of the story. Only witnesses willing to paint the schools in the most despicable colors were allowed to testify. Defenders of the owners were shut off with injunctions like "You are on trial here!" "That is not true. You know it is not true!" The public, said the GOP, should be aware of the unfairness of the Pattison investigation. The Republicans were sure his month long tour of "slander and falsification" would go down as the "darkest page" in the ill-fated history of the Pattison administration. [35]

The Republican press generally concluded its coverage of the Pattison investigation with the same question: "Why did the governor undertake this campaign of vilification?" The answer was politics. It was evident why the governor had taken his attorney general, Lew Cassidy, along on the tour of the schools. As the chief inquisitor of the owners, Cassidy, Pattison's choice to succeed him as governor, would receive much favorable publicity and exposure. [36] It was also reported that reporter Norris, who was the third member of the Pattison investigation, had political ambitions. He had his eye on the lieutenant governorship. [37]

Furthermore, said the Republicans, Democrats were trying to steal an important segment of Republican vote.

"The scheme," cried one Republican editor, "which is as plain as the nose on a man's face is to create in the minds of the GAR a kind feeling towards the Democrats. The GOP editors cautioned the veterans not to be duped by this political maneuver, not "to be drawn over to the party that is endeavoring to perpetuate a joke." The old soldiers were to see the Pattison investigation for what it really was - a cheap Democratic trick to wean the GAR vote away from the party that had saved the Union. [38]

Of course, Pattison's friends denounced these Republican charges. Only minds of the "baser sort" would think that the motives for the investigation were political. "The shoe," said one Pattison spokesman, "pinches these Republican journals on their political corn." To protect the real culprits of their party, the Republicans were trying to hang the millstone of partisanship around the neck of the Democratic governor.

As one Democrat said:

"If the Republican editors suppose they are rendering their party a service by denouncing Governor Pattison, it is to be hoped that they will not be undeceived till the close of the campaign. They should be encouraged to keep on at this sort of thing for they will probably be disillusioned when the Ides of November shall have come." [39]

So, which political party was the most guilty of using the soldiers' orphans to win votes? Soon it became apparent that the issue of the orphans was not rebounding to the advantage of either one. Both the Republicans and the Democrats seemed to be playing politics with the orphans.

What in the spring of 1886 looked like a tactic for political success, later seemed to have all kinds of danger signals. This unpleasant fact acknowledged by a Republican editor could just have well been said by a Democrat:

"The man who attempts to make political capital out of this question will beat his own brains out with a club." [40]

By the fall of the election year, both parties began to back off from the partisan consequences of the alleged "Soldiers' Orphan School Scandal." Other stories like the expose of the GOP "Gas Ring" in Philadelphia, (also written by John Norris of the Record), labor troubles on the nation's railroads, and the marriage of President Cleveland replaced the orphans in the Commonwealth's newspapers.

The Democrats, in particular, did not use the issue to win votes in the gubernatorial election. Their candidate for governor made no mention of the soldiers' orphans in either his acceptance speech at his party's nominating convention or in any of his campaign speeches. [41]

Two explanations can be given for why the Democracy did not use the issue of the orphans. One was the risk of being too closely identified with a partisan issue. In the summer of 1886, both the Grand Army and the adult alumni of the schools, a group called "The Sixteeners," went on record as being opposed to the "partial and partisan investigation" of Governor Pattison. [42] If these groups reflected voter sentiment, the Democrats undoubtedly reasoned that it was best to drop the issue.

Moreover, the candidacy of Pattison's chosen successor, Lew Cassidy, his attorney-general, was not well received by the party. In July, 1886 it was reported that both of them were withdrawing from the political picture. The governor was "taking the waters at Bedford Springs," while Cassidy was on a trip to Europe. Neither took any part in the gubernatorial campaign. [43] Chauncey Black, the Democratic candidate for governor failed to mention the orphans in any of his campaign rhetoric. [44]

After the decline of Governor Pattison's political future, he dropped the issue of the soldiers' orphans for the rest of his term. In the spring, most observers believed Pattison would bring criminal charges against the owners of the schools who had profited unduly from running their school. [45] Indeed he instructed his attorney-general to proceed in the courts against those who had defrauded the state and to "recover some of the ill-gotten gain."[46] But no formal charges were ever made by the Pattison administration. Perhaps it was true as one Republican editor said :

"The state did not prosecute because it knew that there was no case." [47]

Likewise, the Republicans became reticent about the charges connected with the schools. "I prefer to remain quiet," said Republican ex-senator Wright, head of the Syndicate:

"I believe the whole thing will be explained away at the proper time." [48] The newly appointed Inspector of the Soldiers' Orphan Schools, General Louis Wagner, an outspoken critic of the schools, had nothing to say about the outrages. Instead, during the campaign, the influential GOP – GAR leader leader spent his time depreciating the leaders of the long lost Confederacy. [49]

After the Republicans won the election for governor and increased their majority in both houses of the General Assembly, a Republican in the lower house introduced a resolution to investigate the charges made by the former Democratic governor. But it never came out of committee. [50]

In the final analysis, neither Democrats nor Republicans suffered because of the partisan events of 1886. The real losers, as it turned out, were the owners of the schools and the officers of the state Superintendency of the Soldiers' Orphan Schools. The accusations by both parties had so confused the public that the people of the state did not know what to believe. In their confusion, most citizens seemed to believe the worse and doubt the best. As one Republican editor said:

"The disagreements are, to say the least, most unfortunate and to be greatly deplored. If different parties make reports differing so widely the result must inevitably be to create distrust of all." [51]

Due to close in 1890, the fate of the schools, as already pointed out, was decided by the Grand Army. It persuaded the legislature in 1889 to pass a law abolishing the original State Department of the Soldiers' Orphans and establish a new Commission of the Soldiers' Orphans. In July of 1889, the GAR dominated Commission closed five of the private schools. This action, according to one Republican newspaper, was "heartily approved everywhere." [52] No tears were shed for the former and last Superintendent of the old system. The Reverend, Dr. Higbee had been "notoriously weak and inefficient." [53]

The Republican press forgot the defense they had made on behalf of the Republican owners of the schools and the now defunct state Superintendency. Now the GOP editors laughed at and ridiculed the efforts of the owners, particularly the Syndicate, to save their reputations and their schools. [54]

The remaining six private schools never recovered from the events of the "Scandal of 1886." Governor Curtin's patriotic and charitable enterprise established in 1864 was abolished in 1889.

10
The Legacy of the Soldiers' Orphan Schools of Pennsylvania

But for all their failings, the Soldiers' Orphan Schools of Pennsylvania had seemingly served a useful purpose. They had charted a new course in child care which continued long after the original system came to an end. The Commonwealth, indeed, had a right to be proud of this particular "patriotic philanthropy."[1]

In 1881, the real founder of the schools, former Governor Andrew Gregg Curtin, addressed a gathering of former students at the state capitol in Harrisburg. After reviewing the events which had led to the establishment of the schools and congratulating the adult orphans for their good appearance, the governor suggested that the alumni find someone to write a history of the schools, "so that not only the people of the other states of the Union. but nations might know how much Pennsylvania had done to relieve the suffering and horrors of war."[2]

Now, almost a century and a half later, I honor his request.

For the first time in history, a government had come to the direct aid of its soldiers' orphans. No other state had ever at-

Three Chester Springs Boys

tempted such a task.³ Even after nine other northern states had followed the example of Pennsylvania and set up programs to aid their veterans' orphans, the Commonwealth had beat them "all by ten to one."⁴ Those who ran the system claimed that the state spent more money than all the other states combined.⁵ When it finally came to an end in 1889, the state had appropriated nearly ten million dollars for the care of the orphans and over fifteen thousand of them had passed through the schools.⁶

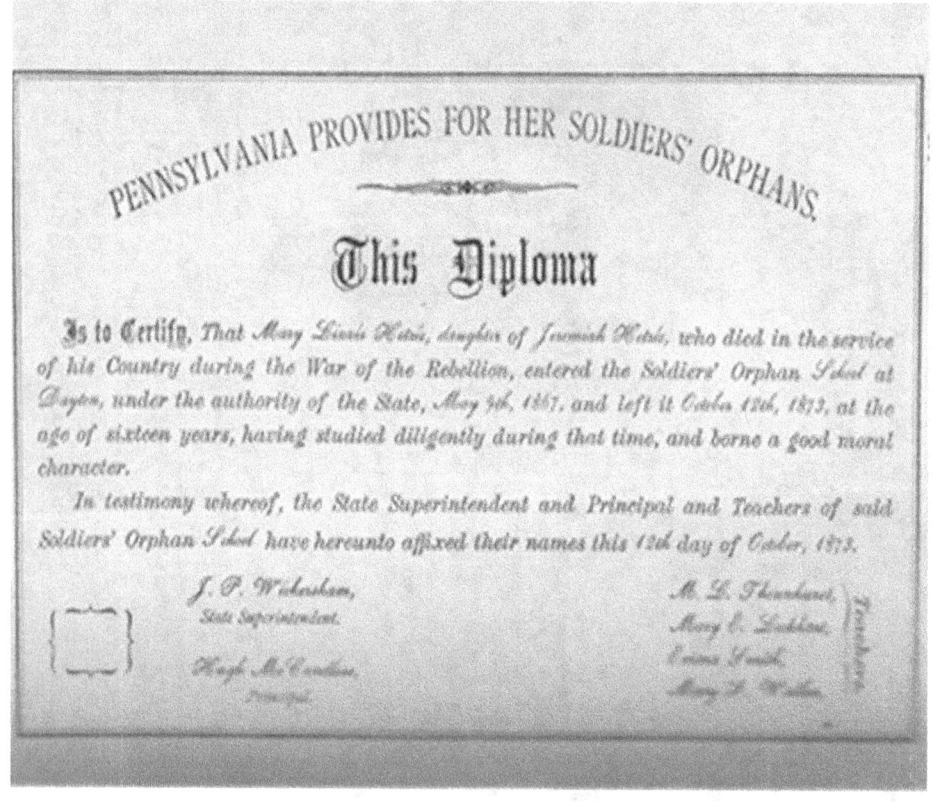

Soldiers' Orphan School Diploma

In comparison, nine other northern states - Illinois, Indiana, Iowa, Kansas, Michigan, Minnesota, Ohio, Wisconsin, and New Jersey had more abbreviated programs. Ohio which after Pennsylvania seemed to have the most ambitious program, spent $160,000 in 1871 to care for 270 orphans, while in the same year

The Keystone State spent three times that amount, $520,000 caring for 3,607 children. In 1889, Michigan spent $100 to care for each of its 200 soldiers' orphans. Pennsylvania's per capita outlay was $175 for each of the its 1800 children. [7]

There was more to the story of the Soldiers' Orphan Schools of Pennsylvania than a comparison with what was done in the other states. The advocates of the Pennsylvania system believed it was serving another purpose. The schools were considered to be experimental educational models. The educators who ran the system claimed they were testing revolutionary pedagogical ideas.

Soldiers' Orphan School, Jumonsville, PA

In 1865, the famous national educational leader, Henry Barnard, was informed by his friend, Thomas Burrowes, the first superintendent of the Pennsylvania Soldiers' Orphan Schools, that at last, the latter would be able to put into practice "some unique educational theories" without running counter to the prevailing "school master prejudice. . .I will be able to introduce a method of instruction . . .which I have I have long been cogitating and maturing but which is not in the books anywhere in operation.[8] "From this experiment of Dr. Burrowes," said a delegate to the Pennsylvania State Teachers' Association convention in 1865, "the highest results are anticipated in reference to our schools generally."[9]

The plan of Dr. Burrowes proved to be less than revolutionary. He claimed he was going to inaugurate a system of industrial education. This, as has been pointed out earlier, turned out to be doing nothing more than simple chores.

One of his ideas, however, was put into practice and seemed to have been followed until 1889. The head teacher in each school supervised the students in a large study hall as they prepared their lessons. Then, the other teachers heard the recitations in smaller adjoining class rooms.

Burrowes' successor as Superintendent, George McFarland, also believed he could use the Soldiers' Orphan Schools to prove the efficacy a new educational idea. McFarland was enthusiastic about turning the prevailing ungraded schools into a graded system. Indeed, he divided the pupils of each school into eight grade levels. In a speech to the state's teachers' convention, McFarland urged that his eight grade plan be adopted in all of the common schools of the state:

"The series of grades that have been very thoroughly tested in the Soldiers' Orphan Schools are applicable in the main to the common schools. Their condition and wants being similar to the Soldiers' Orphan Schools, it is believed similar good results will follow . . ."[10]

There is no evidence that any of the schoolmen in the audience followed McFarland's advice. The majority of the state's schoolhouses remained ungraded through the latter nineteenth century.[11]

Another educator who owned and ran a school was F.A. Allen of the Mansfield Soldiers' Orphan School. Allen was in great demand as a speaker on educational matters. He traveled to teacher conventions as far away as Mississippi and California.[12] Allen called his program "The New Departure." Allen was a great advocate of the "object method" of teaching. Physical objects were used at Mansfield in teaching mathematics and science. Ordinary newspapers were read in the language class.[13] To most schoolmen, however, the Mansfield educator/owner "was in advance of his time."[14] In the general discussion that followed one of his lectures, an English teacher called his ideas "destructive." Another critic said that it was unwise to use newspapers in teaching because of the "danger of partisan politics and parties."[15]

The few innovations associated with the Soldiers' Orphan Schools, while evidently known to the educational profession at large, remained isolated experiments. A check of the debates in Pennsylvania's legislature when changes were made in the common school system - a twenty-day school month, a six month term, free textbooks, compulsory attendance, all of which were in practice in the Soldiers Orphan Schools - reveals no borrowing from the orphan schools.[16] The mandate of the new state constitution of 1873 requiring all children over the age of six to be schooled at public expense was not patterned after the soldiers'

Hoop Drill, Harford School Girls

175

orphan system.[17] Finally, there was nothing in the reports of the state's superintendent of public instruction that suggest this important public official was influenced by what happened in the orphan schools.[18]

The authorities of the Soldiers' Orphan Schools hoped their schools would set a precedent for the care of dependent children. "We wish," said Superintendent Higbee, "that every destitute child within the State had the full advantage of such an education."[19] "What has been done for the soldiers' orphan," seconded Superintendent Wickersham, "must be done for all who need such help."[20] The schools, said defenders of the system, proved that they were no longer in the experimental stage. The state commissioner of public charities claimed that "The Soldiers' Orphan Schools are in all respects fair examples of what can be done for all the hapless children of the state."[21]

The same argument based on social order that was used to rationalize the Soldiers' Orphan Schools was offered to justify a more expanded state program of charitable work. According to one report of the Superintendent of the Orphan Schools, not just fifteen thousand soldiers' orphans, but seventy-five thousand neglected children from all walks of life were "running wild" in the streets of the state. They were "the stuff of which riots and disturbances of the peace" were made. Their destiny was the county almshouse or the state prison, "a tax and plague upon the body politic." The solution was to gather them together as the soldiers' orphans into state schools where they could be trained like the orphans to "good behavior. . .Nor is this mere theory," said Superintendent Wickersham, " My experience with thousands of soldiers' orphans gathered in from homes of destitution, more than proves the position I take." [22]

Street Urchins, late 1800's

Wickersham even prepared a legislative bill to cover the care of all dependent children in the state. Each county would be required to establish a "proper home" patterned on the existing orphan schools for all the "truant, vagrant, and neglected" children in the local district. But, the superintendent's proposal found no support among the lawmakers. It died in committee. Its sponsor hoped that "the day is not far distant when the state will provide for the care of all destitute and dependent children." [23] Except for the soldiers' orphans, the Commonwealth failed to set up institutions for any other orphan children. Well into the twentieth century, the almshouse remained the sanctuary for dependent children. [24]

The Soldiers' Orphan Schools of Pennsylvania seemingly had no influence upon educational and social reform in the later nineteenth century. There is no evidence that new developments in education, a concern for homeless children, and the control by the state of a welfare system common to the Soldiers' Orphan Schools, carried over into the more general educational and social patterns of the state or nation.

The importance of the Soldiers' Orphan Schools of Pennsylvania was that they began something new for the care of a particular type of orphan - the soldiers' orphan. No state had previously set up this kind of child welfare service. In 1865, Superintendent Burrowes was sure that other states would follow the example of Pennsylvania.[25] The next year, Governor Curtin

Rutherford Hayes

revealed that upon request he had forwarded details of the Commonwealth's plan to the governors of Ohio and Connecticut. [26]

Indeed, the governor of Ohio, Rutherford Hayes, acknowledged the leadership of Pennsylvania. At a public meeting in support of establishing a similar plan for Ohio, Hayes noted his state was "sadly behind our sister state." He read a letter from the governor of Pennsylvania explaining how the state had set up its Soldiers' Orphan Schools. Later, the historian of the Ohio system admitted that his state had followed the example of Pennsylvania, the first state to care for soldiers' orphans. [27]

Moreover, it is interesting that nine other states emulated the example of Pennsylvania. But, they did not copy the mistakes and failures of the Keystone state. All of them erected a single school under the direct ownership and operation of the state. There were no private schools. Four of them - Michigan, Illinois, Indiana, and Ohio - initially established bona fide industrial training schools. [28] All of them set up a non-partisan board of directors of Civil War veterans to oversee their schools. [29]

Scotland SOS

Even if a direct connection cannot be made between the Pennsylvania effort and that of the other states, it is clear that the spirit and intent of a century ago lived on in the state of its birth. In 1966, over 500 children of veterans of World War II, the Korean War and the Vietnam War were given institutional care by the state at its 180 acre, 70 buildings of the Scotland School for Veterans' Children.

The state school at Scotland remained in existence until 2009. Then, it was closed due to the state's "budget cuts." It was later sold to the Church of God, which inaugurated a seminary on the site of the soldiers' orphan school.

And so the Soldiers' Orphan Schools of Pennsylvania, 1864-1889 passed into history.

Ruins at Chester Springs School site

Little remains of their presence. At Chester Springs two of the old dormitory buildings still standing house an artists' enterprise. The old school at Mt. Joy was long ago converted into an apartment. At Harford in the northeastern part of the state, the local historical society has restored one of the buildings and gives occasional tours of the restored school.

McAllisterville Academy 2015

Tomb stones in the neighboring hamlets of the schools reveal the burial sites of the orphans who died in the schools.

Grave of Student, Chester Springs

Chester Springs Cemetery Memorial

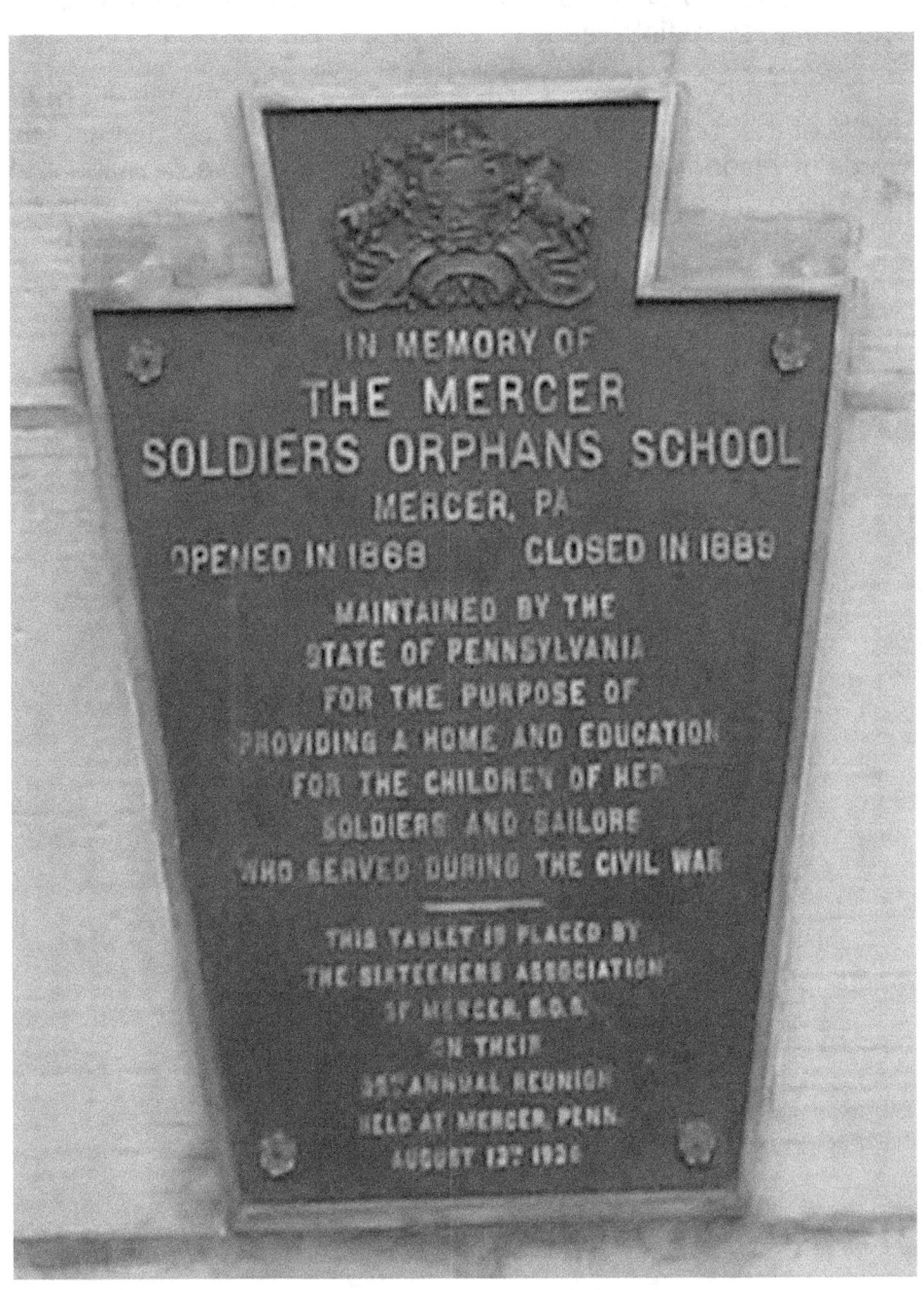

Mercer School Memorial Plaque

Markers show the site of some of the almost forgotten schools. The one in Mansfield reads:

In Memory of Professor F.A. Allen. Erected by the Former pupils of the MANSFIELD SOLDIERS' ORPHAN SCHOOL; His words of wisdom and tender admonition have proved a guide and inspiration. This tablet marks the site of the school, 1867-1889

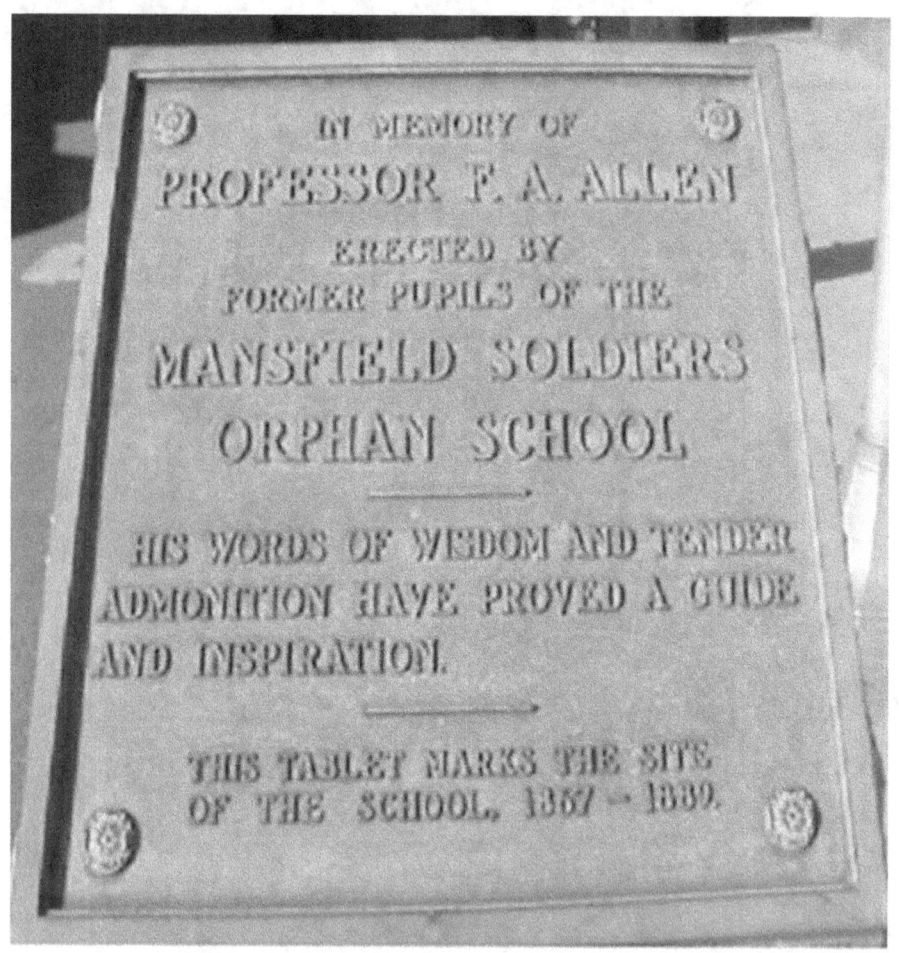

Mansfield School Memorial Plaque

On August 6, 1937 a tablet was erected on the site of the McAlisterville School by the Juniata County Historical Society. One of the brick buildings of this school had been turned into a dress factory. [30]

However, for the most part the Soldiers' Orphan Schools of Pennsylvania, 1864 – 1889 have been forgotten. It was just a minor chapter in the history of the Commonwealth.

But it surely reveals the patriotism and humanitarianism of the latter nineteenth century in the United States. For the first time in the history of the nation, a government took on the care of the children of veterans.

Between 1864 and 1889, thousands of soldiers' orphans passed through the system at a cost of over ten million dollars – Two hundred and sixty-one million in twenty first century funds!

Statue of Andrew Curtin, Gettysburg, P.A.

Certainly the founder of the Soldiers' Orphan Schools of Pennsylvania, Governor Andrew Gregg Curtin, was vindicated:

"I pledged to the brave men when they were about to go into the public service, that if they fell on the field of battle, we would take care of their orphan children. (CHEERS)

Gettysburg

(A VOICE - 'WE WILL')

Just before the battle, I said it to thousands. I said your children shall be protected (CHEERS) I knew that the State so great, so grand, so noble would never turn out these children.

(VOICES - NEVER, NEVER)

One morning when the people gathered in their places of worship, two little ragged children appealed to me for alms as I stepped from my doorway. I learned they were children of soldiers who had fallen in defense of the country. What was my train of thought? I said to myself, is it possible that the people of Pennsylvania , thanking God for victory, can do so when the children of the brave men who brought us the fruits of victory, are on the streets begging for bread! (APPLAUSE)

Street Children of the late 1800's

This beneficence, gentlemen [of the legislature], is the result Pennsylvania has something to be proud of. She has taken the lead in the matter. Other great states have followed her. What a thing to be proud of. All over the Commonwealth, after the greatest war the world has ever seen, I say we have been able to pay our debts and still take care of our soldiers' orphans. No charity of the age and of the past can compare with this. (APPLAUSE)

Girls Calisthenics, Union town School

If you are satisfied, then I ask you to continue this benevolent plan. If you are not satisfied, let the children go.

(VOICES - 'NEVER, NEVER, NEVER')

Examination Day, Chester Springs School

If this body adjourns without doing its duty, let me say gentlemen, I have the power to call you back. (IMMENSE CHEERING) I pray God that the electric spark may fall upon all; that we may all determine to do justice to the poor soldiers' orphans, and that we may thus do ourselves and our great Commonwealth an honor forever!"

(CHEERS)[31]

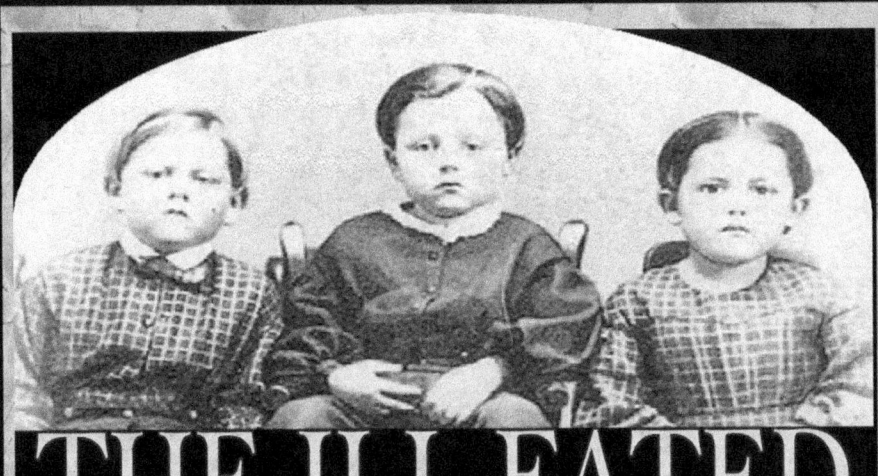

THE ILL-FATED GETTYSBURG ORPHANAGE

Although the Gettysburg orphanage was never part of the state run Soldiers' Orphan School system, it has one of the most dramatic tales of the Civil War Orphanages in Pennsylvania during the same time period. This section features the first publication of the Lunden family letters. Ada, Jimmie and Georgie Lunden resided at the Gettysburg Orphange under the "care" of the notorious headmistress, Rosa Carmichael.

The first publication of the orphan Ada J. Lunden's letter collection

The Ill-Fated Gettysburg Orphanage

It all started with a picture.

FRANK, FREDERICK, ALICE.

The first day of the battle of Gettysburg, July 1, 1863 was disastrous for the Union army. Trying to secure the town of Gettysburg, it was driven in flight by the larger Confederate brigades.

One fleeing blue-clad infantryman, shot in the chest above the heart, realized that his wound was fatal. He collapsed on a vacant lot, took a metal daguerreotype photo from his pocket, and clutching it, gazed for the last time at his three young, soon to be, orphans.

Thus, was born one of the most famous tales of the Civil War - "The Children of the Battlefield."

After the battle, a member of one of the civilian burial details took the photo from the hands of the corpse, marking a temporary grave in case the unidentified soldier would be identified.

"An Incident at Gettysburg" depiction of the fallen father

The "tin-type" of the three orphans came into the possession of a tavern owner outside the town on a road leading into Gettysburg, displayed in the inn, and became a talking point of the community.

Dr. John Francis Bourns, a forty-eight year old physician from Philadelphia, on his way to help treat the thousands of wounded at Gettysburg, stopped at the inn, heard the story of the "Children," and persuaded the inn keeper to give him the daguerreotype. The doctor explained that when he returned to his urban metropolis, he would set in motion a plan to find the three orphans.

By the fall of 1863, the search was underway. First, the doctor had carte de visites, the newly invented paper photos the size of a calling card, copied from the antique daguerreotype. These so-called CDV's were printed by the thousands by the doctor and sent to agents in the northern states for distribution to stores where they were sold to the public for $.25 each. On the back of the picture, Dr. Bourns explained that the proceeds from the sale would be deposited in a fund to secure the future for the yet unidentified widow and her three orphans.

Next, Dr. Bourns went to the metropolitan newspapers of Philadelphia and persuaded the editors to publish the story of the "Children Of the Battlefield."

A particular sentimental and graphic description was printed in the Philadelphia Inquirer of October 19, 1863, headlined "Whose Father Was He?"

"After the battle of Gettysburg, a Union soldier was found in a secluded spot on the field where wounded he laid down to die. In his hands was an ambrotype containing the portraits of three small children. The last object upon which he looked was the image of his children. How touching! How solemn! What pen can describe the emotions of this patriot-father as he gazed upon his children, so soon to be made orphans. His last thoughts are for his family. He has finished his work on earth . He has freely given his life for his country; and, now, with his life's blood ebbing, he clasps the image of his children and, commending them to the

God of the fatherless, rests his last lingering look upon them. The last thoughts of the dying father was for them, and to them only."[1]

Amos Humiston

Since newspapers could not print photographs, the article described the clothing of the children - the older boy and his sister wearing the same patterned material.

The Inquirer article was reprinted in practically every Northern newspaper. On the same day, a widely popular, Philadelphia religious weekly, The American Presbyterian, printed a shorter version of the story.

A copy of this article made its way into the hands of a minister in the small village of Portville in western New York. He knew that one of his young parishoners with three children had not heard from her soldier husband for a couple of weeks. The local postmaster sent this news to Dr. Bourns in Philadelphia. He immediately sent a photo of the three children to Mrs. Philanda Humiston. Her fears were confirmed and the mystery of "The Children of the Battlefield" was solved. The martyred father from Portfield, NY was Sgt. Amos Humiston, of the 154th Regiment of the Army of the Potomac.

The surviving children were Fred, aged four, Frank, eight, and Alice, six.

The now famous Dr. Bourns prepared to make his way to Portville. As the American Presbyterian enthused, "Dr. Bourns proposes to visit Portville and return the ambrotype with his own hands. He is promised an enthusiastic reception. It is hoped that a sufficient sum of money will be raised by the sale of the photograph to give each of the children a good education. Indeed, the idea has suggested to some that the interest occasioned by this beautiful event might be turned to the account of soldiers' orphans generally; and that an effort might be successfully made to found and endow a Soldiers' Orphan Asylum on a large scale. We trust that such may be the result." [2]

For the German Reformed Messenger.

THE CASE OF SERGEANT HUMISTON.

To the Editor of the Ger. Ref. Messenger:

SIR—The history of Sergeant Humiston, and of the effort in progress to provide for the dependent family of the honored soldier, is now known to the country. It is known that the sales of the photograph of the children, have been the simple means relied upon to secure the family's present and prospective support. These sales have been most seriously damaged by a recent counterfeit copy of the photograph, which is being extensively circulated and sold to benefit parties concerned in its issue. The spurious picture comes, or purports to come from New York. This grievous wrong to the widow and orphan children of the fallen soldier ought to be held up to the indignation of the public.

The humane and patriotic, desiring to assist in paying the debt the country owes to this stricken family, will be glad to learn that the genuine copies of the orphans' photograph are now executed only in Philadelphia, and have upon them a printed statement of the object of their sale, with the imprint of the several Philadelphia artists who furnish them.

The amount thus far realized for the family is not quite fourteen hundred dollars. It is not intended to enrich this soldier's family, to the neglect of families of other soldiers who have perished in defence of the Union; but after suitably providing for the Humiston orphans, any profits arising from continued sales of their picture, and of the music just published, shall be appropriated to the relief of other orphaned families, having an equal claim to the country's grateful sympathy and protection.

I am, sir, respectfully yours,

J. FRANCIS BOURNS.

Philadelphia, May 28th, 1864.

☞ Genuine copies of the photograph referred to in the foregoing note from Dr. Bourns, may be had at the Bookstore of Mr. S. S. Shryock, Chambersburg. Price 25 cents for small size, and 75 cts for large.

The conquering hero, Dr. Bourns, presented a check of $55.00 to the unfortunate widow.

The tragedy of Amos Humiston and "The Children of the Battlefield" and its resolution became one of the sensational news stories of the Civil War. It caught the imagination and sympathy of the people of this later 19th century Romantic era.

The latter part of the American Presbyterian article reveals how the leading light of the whole episode, Dr. Bourns, was going to change the emphasis of his crusade. The public was informed that the funds raised by the sale of the CDV's were now going to be used to establish an orphanage for all the soldiers' orphans of the Civil War.

The American Presbyterian sponsored a contest for the best poem about the three orphans. A popular songwriter, J.G. Clark, won the contest and his ballad, "The Children of the Battlefield," became one of the musical hits of the era. Usually, sheet music sold for 25 cents but this one was priced at 50 cents - the profits going to Dr. Bourns and the projected orphanage. As with the photo, the doctor penned a note on each of the compositions:

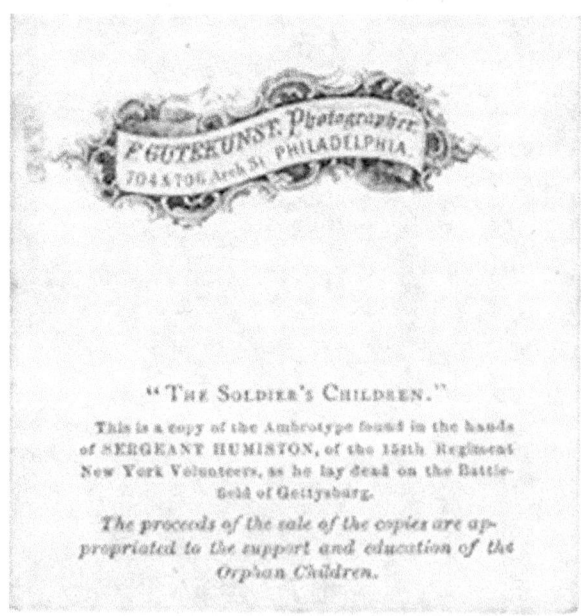

The Children of the Battlefield Sheet Music

"The copies are sold in furtherance of the National Sabbath School effort to found in Pennsylvania an asylum for dependent orphans of soldiers . . . This [song and picture] is private property and may not be copied without wronging the Soldiers' Orphans for whom it was published. Philadelphia, Sept 23, 1865, J. Francis Bourns.[3]

The reference to the "Sabbath Schools" was an astute marketing ploy developed by the doctor and the editor of the religious journal. Sunday School classes subscribed $25.00 for the establishment of the Soldiers' Orphans at Gettysburg. Each Sunday School would become a trustee of the worthy institution. The dimes and nickels of the children of the Sunday Schools rolled into Dr. Bourns and his organization, The National Orphans' Homestead Association, of which the doctor was general secretary, treasurer and all around guiding light. Such famous Americans as former President, James Buchanan, Generals Grant and Mead, and financiers, Jay Gould and Jay Cooke, donated funds and inscribed their names as benefactors.

To much fanfare, the Homestead for Soldiers' Orphans opened in November, 1866. Fifteen boys and ten girls were the first "inmates." Philinda and her three children left New York and became residents at the Homestead.

The mother became the wardrobe custodian and seamstress at the new orphanage.

Philadelphia, Oct. 13,
1868

To the Scholars of Willow Street
School, Norristown, Pa.
Dear Children,
It gives me very great
pleasure to acknowledge your
contribution of one hundred and
fourteen dollars & eighty-seven
cents ($114.87), to the Nation-
al Homestead at Gettysburg
for Orphans of our Soldiers
and Sailors. Though the
money was raised, as I learn,
by means of a Fair, we must
feel that we owe the very
pleasing surprise of its
receipt entirely to yourselves.
One who knew similar
efforts in behalf of the

1868 Letter from Bournes

Little is known about the actual operation of this private orphanage set up for the soldiers' orphans from eleven northern states. The girls evidently learned the domestic skills of housekeeping and sewing. The boys did chores around the institution and worked in the garden in the summer.

As with most philanthropic institutions of the day, grand events at the Homestead on Christmas, Thanksgiving, and Memorial Day were noted in the local press. The celebration of Washington's birthday in 1868 was typical:

"A pleasant reception took place at the National Orphans' Homestead on Saturday afternoon. The large school room was crowded with visitors. An illuminated motto, "God Bless Our Home" spanned the entrance. The Orphans, 60 in number (35 girls and 25 boys) were seated on an elevated platform - the girls wearing blue dresses with white sashes and shields with the names of the various states emblazoned thereon, the boys wearing either shields or miniature flags. The decorations were all in good taste. The exercises opened with Prof. Ferrier [from the College], followed by a poetical recitation, "Salutation of the Flag," the production of Miss Lattiner [the teacher at the orphanage], in which four of the children participated. Major Cleeton, the New England agent of the Home, read an essay, "The Boyhood of Washington" and Lieut. Norton (the superintendent of the orphanage), an original poem by Miss Lattimer, "The Drunkard's Wife." This was followed by an allegorical tableaux of the 13 original states, "Tribute to Washington," an original production by Miss Lattimer. Remarks were made by Prof. Ferrier and D. McConaughy, Esq. (a local attorney) while Maj. Cleeton gave some interesting details of his experiences as an Agent of the Home. The exercises were interspersed with frequent singing by the children, closing with the national hymn, "America, Tis' of Thee." At the close of the exercises, the Zouaves under Capt. Norris drilled for half an hour or more much to the gratification of the Orphans." [4]

The Homestead seemed to prosper during its early years. Those in charge seemed to be competent and energetic. One of the superintendents was a former officer in Amos Humiston's old military outfit. The staff included the Superintendent and his wife, a matron supervising the girls and a male attendant who

The Humiston Children while living at the Homestead

was in charge of the boys, a housekeeper, a cook, a handyman and a wardrobe attendant. It remained solvent as over 700 Sunday Schools throughout the nation, each subscribed $25.00 each year. Wealthy entrepreneurs continued to fund the institution, some even sending gifts to the Homestead:

"Misses Evans and Watson of Philadelphia," The Gettysburg Star and Sentinel reported, "have sent to the National Orphans' Homestead a donation of a fireproof safe . . .and it is a very fortunate gift." [5]

1867 photograph of Generals Grant, Carter and Porter and Governor Geary during their visit to the Homestead

Petitions from important benefactors of the orphanage found their way to Congress:

"We see it stated that on Monday, a meeting of the Senate Committee of Military Affairs, a petition from Bishop Simpson, General Meade, George H. Stuart, Jay Cooke and others was

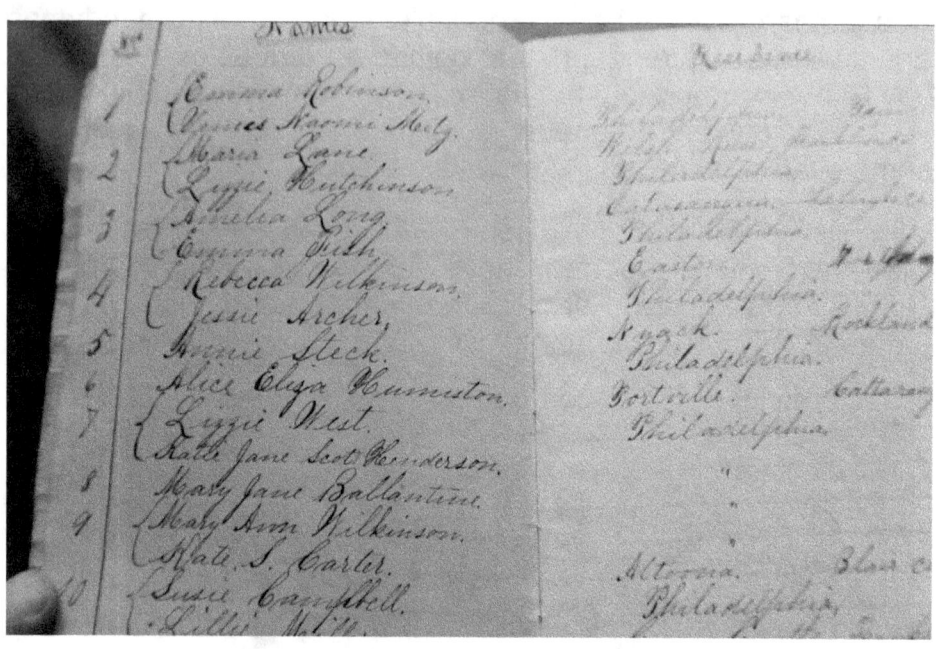

School Roster kept by Mrs. Humiston and Frank Humiston

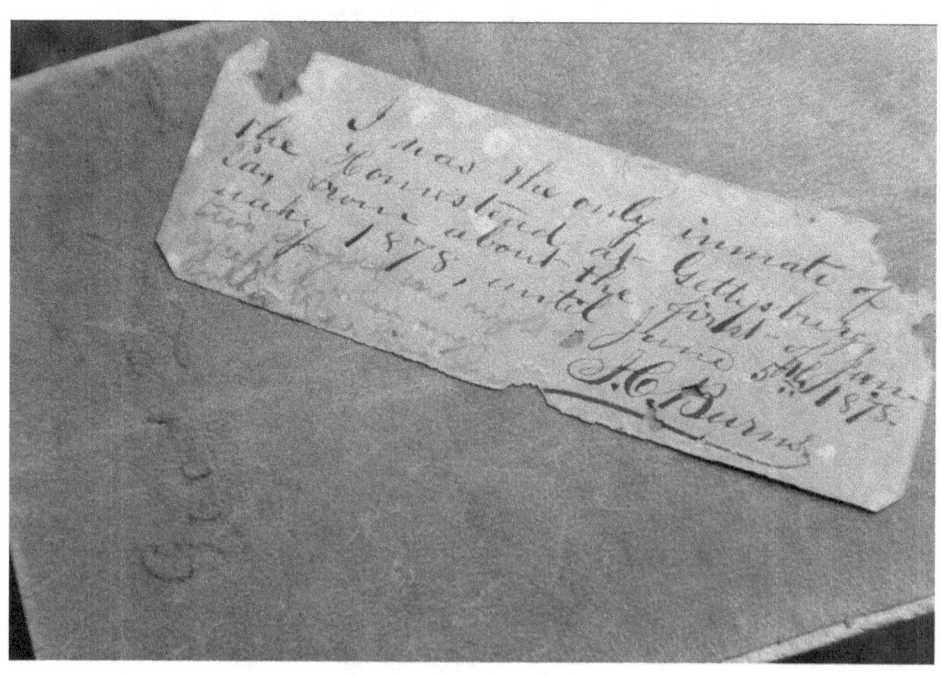

Student's Journal

read asking for Congressional aid to the Soldiers' National Orphan Homestead at Gettysburg and that the Committee agreed to report a bill giving the institution $25,000."[6]

Unfortunately, the bill did not become law.

The community of Gettysburg was proud of its benevolent institution: "It may be confidently asserted," said the Homestead Journal of November, 1869, "that what has been thus far done, has been well done. Why more has not been accomplished and the Homestead is no greater blessing is readily known. Eight acres of ground is owned on Cemetery Hill, and our buildings, though not large are complete. By dint of hard work and rigid economy in expenditures, under God, the treasury is able to meet all current demands and is free of debt. The generous contributions, especially from the Sabbath Schools, continue to flow in. Seven hundred schools in eighteen states, belonging to every branch of the Christian Church, are now shareholders in the Homestead and are co-workers in building this Children's monument of the Nation's Gratitude.

The school is now in a state of advanced excellence. Few boarding schools for boys and girls could be found to excel it. Very few of the pupils now require to be driven.

The religious culture of the children continues to receive zealous and prayerful attention. Family worship morning and evening is never omitted, and the children regularly attend public worship in the town on the Lord's Day.

The sanitary conditions of the Institution could hardly be improved. From the start in 1866, there has not occurred a single case of serious protracted sickness.

Shall not the work be urged more rapidly forward, and the Institution become a far greater blessing? It ought to be. It could be. And we have the faith to believe it shall be."[7]

"We are pleased to see a growing interest in the Homestead on the part of our citizens. Such an institution is an honor and a blessing to any community," enthused the Gettysburg Star and Sentinel in 1870.[8]

Design for the Expansion of the Orphanage

In 1875, Dr. Bourns wrote to a friend, "Within a day or two past, I received account of the good health of the Homestead family." [9]

Little did the doctor realize, however, that the clouds of disaster were beginning to appear over the Soldiers' Orphans' Orphanage of Gettysburg.

Mrs. Humiston, evidently, had never been happy at the Homestead. In 1869, she married a Massachusetts minister and left the orphanage.

The following year, Dr. Bourns hired a new superintendent, Mrs. Rosa Carmichael. In his report to the Association board of Directors, he wrote, "As a teacher and disciplinarian, Mrs. Carmichael has few equals, and she is a most assiduous and faithful worker, laboring often beyond her strength in school and out."

Rosa Carmichael

As it turned out, however, to most critics of the time and modern commentators, the coming of Mrs. Carmichael proved to be the eventual undoing of the Gettysburg institution.

THE LUNDEN FAMILY LETTERS 1870 – 1876 [10]

There are few surviving documents which chronicle the daily life of the children "inmates" of the Gettysburg Orphanage and the experience of their widowed mothers. The Lunden family letters are a rare example. This is the first time these letters have been published. They are found in the Wade Hall Collection of American Letters: Ada Jane Lunden (accession-call# 2009ms132.0172) University of Kentucky Special Collections Research Center.

Between 1870 and 1976, two to all three of Sarah Lunden's "orphaned" children resided at the Gettysburg Orphanage. This was during the reign of Mrs. Rosa Carmichael as headmistress. She was later charged with the assault and battery of Georgie Lunden.

It appears from the originals that the letters from the children to their mother are censored and corrected. In some cases, the letters from her son are entirely composed by Dr. Bourns.

Page from the 1870 Census of the Gettysburg includes Frank Humiiston and Sadie Farley

1870

The Road into Gettysburg, 1870

Homestead Orphanage, Gettysburg PA, May 11th 1870
My Dear Mother,
Jimmie received you kind and welcome letter and was glad to hear from you. I am well and hope you are enjoying the same health.
It is a very rainy day and we can not go out and play.
We enjoy ourselves very much. I send my love to you all.
The blossoms are on the trees and it looks very nice. The boys all play "Shimmy" and "Pig in the Pen" and "Hafby Hafby" and some more plays.
I will send you three more cards that I got for getting under Good. Mr. and Mrs. Hilton are both well and send their love to you.
We have sewing hour in the afternoon for the large girls and on Tuesdays and Friday the little girls.

Please come to see me. We would be very glad to see you. I will write to Jennie and Carrie Clark next week.

I can not think of much this time, but I will try and think of more the next time I write. I do not play with my doll. I want to see how nice I can keep it for I want to play with it when I come home.

I sit in the seat with Sadie Farley and Addie Snope in school I will close by saying Good Bye.

from your loving daughter,
Ada Lunden
(Note: Ada was ten years of age.)

Hollidaysburg, PA June 13th, 1870

My Dear Little Children,

I received my little daughter's letter and was so glad to hear from you. We are all well. I am glad you enjoy yourselves so much. It is very nice to have ripe cherries now. Ours is not ripe yet. I am coming down to see you before long and I will bring Georgie with me but I will write again and tell you when I am coming. Aunt Sue sends love to you both and says she would like to see you. Grandpap, Grandma and Aunt Mill sends love to Ada and Jimmy. I think I will close my letter for tonight as I am tired and it is late. My love to my dear Little ones from Your Loving Mother, Sarah Lunden

Hollidaysburg August 14, 1870

My Dear Little Children,

I received Jimmy's or rather Mr. Bourns Letter and am certainly very grateful to him for writing to me for I was getting a little uneasy for I had not had a letter from either of you for a long time. I did not write sooner for I wanted to tell you when I was coming.. You may expect me down the last of next week. I cannot tell you just what day I will come. I will bring Georgie with me. Elmer Gibson's mother came to see me this week and said I should tell you to tell Elmer she thought she would be down to see him next week. I will not write much for I hope I will see you soon if nothing happens. I will close with lots of love to my dear little ones.

Your Loving Mother, Sarah Lunden

Henrietta, PA September 1870

My Dear Little Grand Daughter

I received yours and was glad to hear you was well and have so many kind friends and enjoying yourselves so well. Give my love to Jimmy. You want to know how to make cheese…scald the milk. I can tell you better when you all come home to see us. Grandpa and Will send their love to you.

My mind wanders and I can't write.

From your Grandma to Ada Lunden , my love to you both.

Hollidaysburg Dec 11th 1870

My Dear Little Daughter,

I received your Dear welcome Little Letter. I was so glad to get it for I had not had a letter from you for about a month. I began to wonder what had become of my little girl…. You asked if I remember those little girls. I don't just exactly remember what any of them looked like only Bonnie Peters and she talked to me more than the others did when I was there but I remember all the little children in the house every night in my Prayers. I am going to send you a box I think I will get it off the middle of next week but I will write to you at the time I send your box. It is pretty cold here.,,, we have had nice weather till now and it is snowing today …the ground is white. Ada I always forget to tell you when I came home I went to see Mrs. Banks and gave her the Pin Lap you sent her. She was very much pleased. She thinks you can sew nicely and I gave the little one to Annie Bayley and she thinks it is so nice. She was (asking) me today when you was coming home. I have a class in Sunday school with eight little girls and they are very much interested about you. They say you must go to see them all when you come home. I think I will close my letter for this time….tell Jimmy I will answer his letter as soon as I can. Grandpa, Grandma and your Aunties send love to Ada and Jimmy. I will close with love to all the little ones and much love to my ones.

Your Loving Mother,
Sarah Lunden

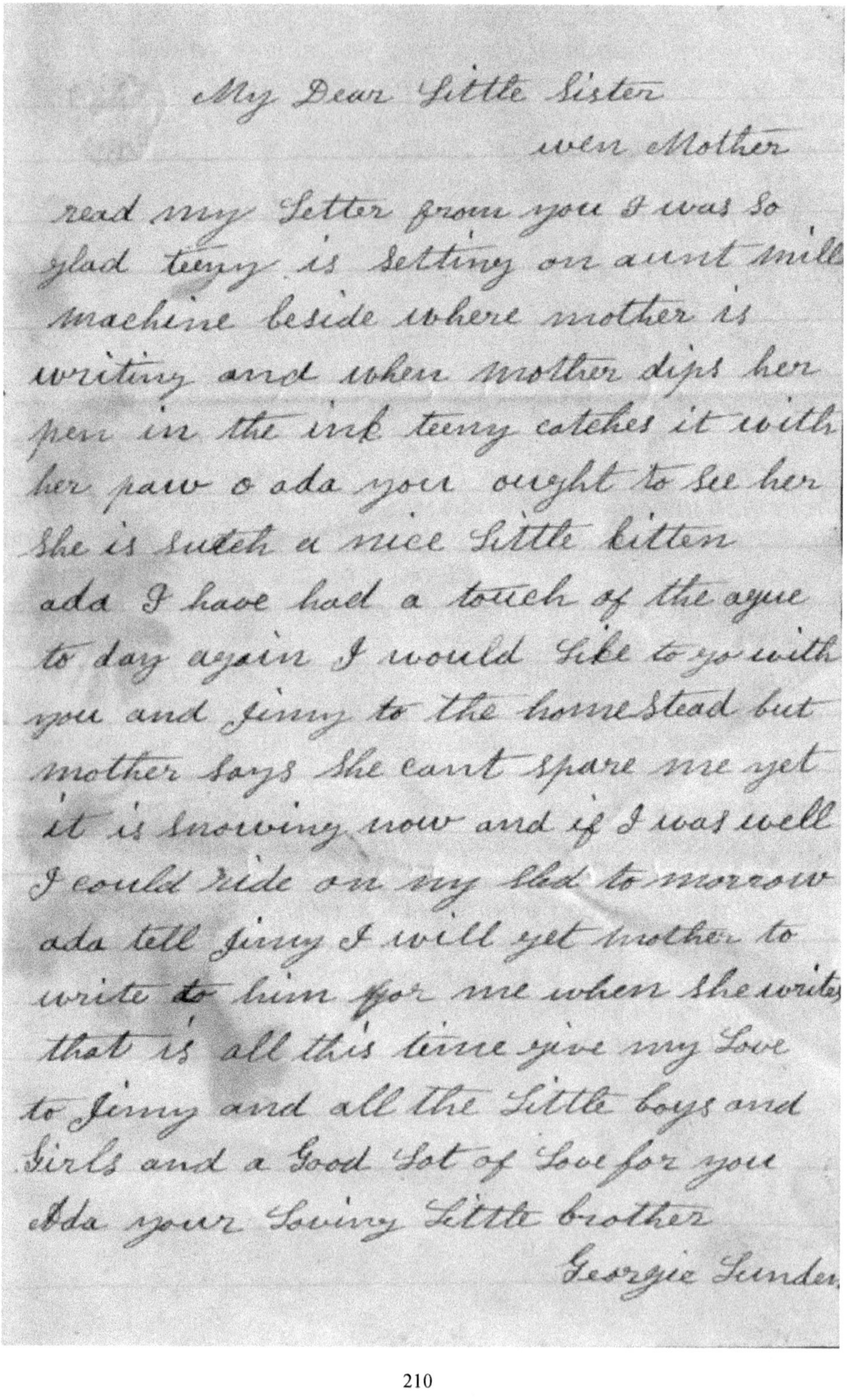

My Dear Little Sister

wen Mother read my Letter from you I was so glad teeny is setting on aunt mill machine beside where mother is writing and when mother dips her pen in the ink teeny catches it with her paw o ada you ought to see her she is sutch a nice Little kitten ada I have had a touch of the ague to day again I would Like to go with you and Jinny to the homestead but mother says she cant spare me yet it is snowing now and if I was well I could ride on my sled to morrow ada tell Jinny I will get mother to write to him for me when she writes that is all this time give my Love to Jinny and all the Little boys and Girls and a Good Lot of Love for you Ada your Loving Little brother

Georgie Sunder

My Dear Little Sister,

When Mother read my letter from you I was so glad. Teeny (the kitten) is sitting on Aunt Mill('s) machine beside where mother is writing and when mother dips her pen in the ink Teeny catches it with her paw. Ada you ought to see her! She is such a nice little kitten. Ada I have had a touch of the ague today again. I would like to go with you and Jimmy to the Homestead but mother says she can't let me yet. It is snowing now and if I was well I could ride on my sled tomorrow. Ada tell Jimmy I will get Mother to write to him for me when she writes. That is all this time.. give my Love to Jimmy and all of the little boys and girls and a good lot of love for you Ada.

Your Loving Little Brother,
Georgie Lunden

1871

The Gettysburg Homestead Orphanage

Hollidaysburg, Feb 16th, 1871

My Dear Little children

I received two letters – one from each of you. They was both in one envelope They came from your Grandma Lunden. They had been directed to her to Altoona. Now Ada, I don't like it very much. I want you to address my letters to me. You spoke of you and Annie Stark writing to me. I did not get them. Those two I have just received is the first I have had since the seventh of December from you. I began to think my two little ones had forgotten their own dear Mother and little brother. Ada you don't know how glad I was to get your letters. Give my love to Annie and tell her I did not get her letter. She will have to write it over and send it. Grandma sends two envelopes, one for Ada and one for Jimmy. This is all.

Good night from your loving mother
Sarah Lunden

My Dear Little Brother and Sister,

I am well and I have had no letter from you for a long time. Jimmy, I am saving my money and when you come home next summer Mother is going to give you some money and you and me is going up the street to buy a squil shooter and Ada can buy something too. Won't that be nice. Mother was out at Aunt Martha's two weeks and I was nearly dead to her. I send my love to all the little girls and boys. Jimmy, I have a whole lot of marbles and when you come home we can play. Mother is going to put her letter and mine in my envelope. Grandma gave it to me and she is sending you and Ada one just like mine. I am getting sleepy. I want to go to bed. Good night and lots of love to my little brother and little sister your brother, Georgie Lunden

Hollidaysburg, March 6th, 1871

My Dear Little Daughter,

I received your dear little letter, it was so very dear to your Mother. I almost thought you had forgot me. I was so glad to hear you and Jimmy was both well and happy. I am also glad to hear from Letty and Bella. Give my love to them and all the best to the little girls and boys. I am glad you was pleased with your bow that Grandma Lunden sent you. You have never told me whether you got the bow I sent you or not. I should like very much to know. Ada I am very much pleased with your writing, it is so plain. I want you to tell me when you write again if Jimmy writes his own

letters. Ada, I met Elmer Gibson and his Mother last Saturday on the street and she wants to send Elmer back to the homestead. But she says his Guardian told her they would not take him back. I told her I was surprised that she had kept him home so long. But she says he was so sick so long after he came home. And I told her to write to Philadelphia to Dr. Bourns about it and she wanted me to mention it in my letter to you. Let your teachers read this. Tell Jimmy to write to Mother whenever it comes his turn. Ada in this letter you will find two little ribbons. Your Aunt Mill sends them to you to dress your doll with. Georgie is well he is in bed fast asleep now. I think I will close for this time with lots of love to my little son and daughter. Your loving Mother
 Sarah Lunden

Hollidaysburg April 3rd, 1871
 My Dear Little Girl,
 I received your nice long letter. How nice it is to get so long a letter from my little daughter. I think you are improving so much in your writing. Ada, I wish you would tell me in your next letter if Jimmy can write any yet. I have not had a letter from him for a long time. I would like to hear from my little boy sometimes. I am

glad you enjoy yourselves so much and so you are counting the months you stay there. It is just three months till you come home. Well, the time will soon go around. Ada, your Aunt Amelia has got some more nice ribbons for you but I will keep them till you come home. Ada, I had a letter from Margret Allen last week she wants to hear how you and Jimmy are getting along. I must answer her letter. Georgie is well. He is gone to bed. He goes to school and learns very fast. He can read a little in the speller. We are all well except Grandpap. He has a very bad cold. We all send love to you and Jimmy. Give my love to all the little girls. It is 9 o'clock and I must bid you all good night with much love to my dear little ones. I am your affectionate Mother.
    Sarah Lunden

Homestead Orphanage, Gettysburg, PA April 26, 1871
    Dear Mother,
    I received the last letter you wrote to me and was very glad to hear from you. Last Wednesday all the children went to a show and I saw lions and tigers, camels, elephants, monkeys, a kangaroo and a great many other things. Jimmie and I are both well and hope you are the same. I will write a little letter to Jennie and Carrie Clark if I can. I will now close so Good Bye. From your daughter, Ada Lunden
    Write soon

Hallidaysburg May 15th 1871
    My Dear Little Daughter,
    I received your letter and was glad to hear from my little ones. I should have answered it sooner but did not have time. We are all well. You tell me you have been to another animal show and seen so many nice things and I think your teachers are so very kind. You ought to be very obedient children and try to do everything they tell you. Ada, I had a letter from Margret Allen and she wanted to know how you and Jimmy was getting along and sends her love to both of you. My Dear Little ones it will not be long now till vacation …only six or seven weeks when I hope to have my three little ones with me. I have been looking for a letter from Mrs. Woods for the last week about your coming home but have received none yet. She said she would write to Mr. J.C. Bourns and she would let me know all about it when she got an answer. Your

little brother is very well and he is getting so tall you and Jimmy will hardly know him when you come home. He sends love to Ada and Jimmy and all the little boys and girls. Give my love to all the children. I will close with Lots of love to my dear Little Boy and Girl... Good bye from your loving Mother.
Sarah Lunden

Hallidaysubrg, July 17th 1871

My Dear Little Daughter,

I received your letter and I was glad to hear you had such a nice time on the Fourth of July. I cannot say so much for us. The fire company of this place had a picnic. All the fire companies from Altoona was here. There was a great many people in town and your cousins Annie, Molly, Frank and Harry came to spend the fourth with us. Well. we got our dinners ready and went to the grove where the picnic was and we eat our dinners and then it began to rain very hard and everybody runs to try and get a shelter. But could not find any and we were all wet to the skin. That was what happened here on the Fourth. You say you would like to see me and I would dearly love to see my two dear little ones but I cannot for a while yet. We are all well. John Lunden was here today He says he would like so much to see you. George has had the ague this summer again but he is better now. He is in bed fast asleep. He will answer your letter sometime. Again, it is getting late and they are all in bed but me. So, I will have to close Good Night from your Loving Mother
Sarah Lunden
PS So very Much love for Jimmy and Ada.
Ada, tell Mr. Bourns I am very much obliged to him for answering my letters from Jimmie

Hollidaysburg, September 6th , 1871

My Dear Little Children,

I have received your letters and you must forgive mother for not answering them soon. I suppose you will wonder where I got this paper. Well your cousin George W. Martin and his wife and his two little children, your little cousins Lincoln and Milly are here on a visit from Junction City Kansa. George and them are having a nice time. Ada may look for a letter from her own mother next week. I have been so very busy I could not write to anybody. Grandma has been out at Aunt Martha's for about three weeks and we have all the work to do and our serving to attend. So you see I am kept very busy. I think Grandma will be home some time this week. I am going to send my little girl and boy some thing nice next week or the week following. I can't tell which now but you will see it when it come. It is bedtime and I must close with lots of love to my dear little pets Ada and Jimmy from your own Mother, Sarah Lunden

Hollidaysburg, September 23, 1871
My Dear Little Daughter,

I received your and my little Jimmy's letters . I am always so glad to hear from you. You say you did not have a letter from me for a long time. I could not help it. Your cousin George and his family are here yet and I have been so busy. Ada, I suppose you have been looking for what I was going to send you. Well, I intended to send you some Grapes and I went to Mr. West to get a box and he persuaded me not to send them. He said it would cost me more than they was worth. He said if I would send you 50 cts, it would buy you as many Grapes as you could eat. I am so sorry I can't send them but I will send you 25 cts a piece to buy whatever you want. Give Jimmy his 25 cts to do what he pleases with. In this letter you will find two pieces of your cousins George's writing paper. One is for Ada and one for Jimmy. I believe that is all. We are all well. Much love to my little Daughter and Son. Ada, I am very anxious to know what it is you have for your Mother. Give my love to your teachers and the children. From you Loving Mother
Sarah Lunden

Homestead Orphanage, Gettysburg, PA September 27, 1871
My Dear Mother,

I received your kind and very pleasant letter and was very glad to hear from you. We are both well and hope you are the same. If you come to see us I will tell you what I have for you ... but I guess I will tell you any how. It is a handkerchief and a cake of sope. I have a wissel for Georgie. I bought a one cent prize bag and that wissel was in it and I told Lizzie Bortz I was going to keep it for brother George. Please send me my little earrings and some patches and silks for my doll and a pair of sissors and please send them up with Grandmother Lunden. We would like to see you all very much. Jimmie and I will send you card ... it is not

like the cards Mr. Hilton gave out to those that was under good. Mr. Supler gave us these cards, you must tell me you received the card and good bye from your daughter
    Ada Lunden
    Write soon sooner soonest

Hollidaysburg October 23 1871
    My Dear Little Children
    I received all of your letters. Jimmy wants to know if I got the cards. Tell him I did and I am going to take good care of them. It is the first (report) card I have had from Jimmy. It makes me think he is a very good boy to get such a card as that. Ada, I did not get the cards in your letter. I got them in Jimmy's and I got one in Jimmy's last letter. Ada, I am very much pleased with the present you have for me and Georgie is delighted about his whissel. I will send you some patches as soon as I get a chance. Georgie was up to the mountain to Grandma Lundens and we had a nice time running through the woods hunting chestnuts. I will send you some when I send your box. Your Cousin George Martin and his family have… gone home to Junction City. We felt so sorry to see them go so far away. I must close my letter to write one for Georgie. With much love I remain your affectionate Mother
    Sarah Lunden

    My Dear Little brother and sister,
    I am well and so is mother. We was away to Grandma Lundens and had a nice time. Ada and Jimmy – we have the nicest little kitten and we call it Gypsie and it runs and plays all around the house and it sleeps in Mother's work basket. Jimmy, I will send you some marbles as soon as I can. I will put a blue and red feather in this letter for Ada's dolls hat. I found them. I would like so much to see my brother and sister for I get so lonesome sometimes. Mother says she wants me to learn to read this winter. This is all this time. To Ada and Jimmy Lunden from their loving brother,
    Georgie

Hollidaysburg, November 13th, 1871
    My Dear Little Children,

I received your letters and am always glad to hear from you. Ada, you want a shawl. I will send you one in your box when I send it. I can not send it soon for I have not the money to buy you one yet. I have your kitten Teeny yet and Gypsie is her kitten. I had a letter from your Cousin George since he left us and he says they arrived home safe and all well. We are all well and hope this will find my two little darlings and all the rest the same. Georgie is well and sends so very much love to his brother and sister….. Ada, enclosed you will find a very nice piece of poetry you must let Jimmy read it too. I will close for this time with love for Ada and Jimmy your affectionate Mother,
    Sarah Lunden

Homestead Orphanage, Gettysburg December 19, 1871
    Dear Mother,
    I received your kind letter and was very glad to hear from you. I am well and hope you are the same. The girls are going to have some pieces on Christmas night and Ada is in some of the pieces. The leaves are all off the trees. This is all I have to say. So goodbye from your affectionate son,
    Jimmie Lunden, Inmate No. 52

THE WINE-CUP.

Young man, that cup of sparkling wine,
    Just lifted to thy lip!
Heed well the fate that may be thine
    If that vile draught you sip;
A maniac's death, a drunkard's grave,
In thoughtless mirth you madly brave.

A prison's gloom, a felon's name,
    A murderer stained with blood,
A life of woe, a death of shame,
    I see within its purple flood;
Drink, then, that cup of sparkling wine,
Young man, and these may all be thine.

The widow's wail, the orphan's cry,
    The frenzied maniac's yell,
The bloated cheek, the blood-shot eye
    Are all within the wine cup's spell;
It flings o'er life a rayless gloom,
And kills for aye beyond the tomb.

Then taste no more the sparkling cup,
    An adder's tooth is in the wine;
A simoon's blast to wither up
    All hope of bliss that may be thine;
But as a serpent, from thee throw
The cup that brings but shame and woe.

Clipping from Sarah

Gettysburg
Dec 13th 1871

Dear Mother
I received your kind letter and was very glad to hear from you I am well and and hope you are the same the girls are going to have some plays on christmas night and Ada is in it some of the pacis the leaves are all of off the tres this is all I have to say so good by from your obedient son

Jimmie Lowden
No 52

1872

Hollidaysburg Jan 23rd 1872
    My dear Little Son and Daughter,
    I received your letter and was very glad to get it. I wanted to hear if you got your box safe. I am glad you are pleased with what was in it. Ada, you want to know who sent you the doll. It was your own mother and I want you to take good care of it so if you come home next summer you can have it nice to bring with you. I should like to have been at the Home on Christmas to see you little folks enjoying yourselves. I am sure you must have had a nice time. I should like you to tell me all about it when you write. Georgie is well and sends his love to his brother and sister. He sends a paper in this letter for Ada. He says you must cut those dolls out and dress them. It is all he has to send. They have been lying around till they have got dirty. He wants you to tell him in his next letter if you dressed them. He wants me to tell you his little kitten Gypsie is dead and he is so sorry about it. But Teeny is all right. She is lying on my lap as I am writing this letter. I hope this will find you all well as it leaves us. Your Grandma Lunden was here last week and she says she don't know what is the reason you don't write to her. Ada you ought to write to her once in a while. I will now close with much love to my little boy and girl. Your Loving Mother,
    Sarah Lunden

Homestead Orphanage, Gettysburg Pa. Feb 14, 1872
    Dear Mother,
    Jimmie wrote you a letter last week…
    Please ask Willie to write me, and tell me how he is getting along and if he goes to school any more. Tell Georgie that I have some marbles for him. When you write next time please tell me if this letter interested you.
    On Friday we say pieces of poetry, and I would like very much if you could send me some poetry.
    I received a letter from Grandma Lunden, and she said perhaps she would come up to see us this spring and she also said that she was out at Aunt Rachel's when you sent our box and if she had known it, she would have put something in for us. She sent us 25 cts each.

I am getting along right well with my lessons 'section C' is the class I am in.

I would like to see you all very much.

Please ask Jennie and Carrie Clark why they don't write to me anymore. I would like to hear from them very much.

Hatie Carter is well, and sends her love to you all. Some pleasant evenings. Mrs. Carmichael, our teacher, takes the girls down on the porch and plays with them.

So good bye from your affectionate Daughter
Ada Lunden
Write soon

Dear Brother

You will answer my last letter next time Mother writes. Georgie, I dressed those paper dolls up you told me I think they were very nice. I am very sorry your kitten is dead. I guess you are very sorry yourself. Jimmy has a cold and he has a frog in his throat as you us[e] to say when you caught like he does now.

Good bye from your sister
Ada Lunden

Paper dolls, early 1870's

Hollidaysburg March 18th 1872
My dear Little Children

I have answered Jimmy's letter and I now sit down to answer yours. Ada you tell me Jimmy wrote a long letter on the slate. I do wish he had wrote it on paper to me. You and Jimmy's letters are so interesting to me. I do love to read them so. And Ada, the last letter I had from you is the most interesting one I have had yet and I am so much pleased with those cards. They show that you are trying to be a good girl and learn all you can. Willie is not at home now only over Sunday. He is driving a milk wagon for a man in Dunesville and he stays there all the week. I am going to send you some poetry. I want you to tell me in your next letter which piece you think is the nicest. I seen Carrie Clark and she says she wrote to you last but she would write to you again. Give love to Katie Carter tell her I have not seen her mother for a long while. There is several cases of small pox in town yet. There is a man only two doors from us that has it. Sam Lasher is his name. He is Fanny Robesons brotherinlaw. You know Fanny Ada. We are all well now. I will close my letter with lots of love to my Little Son and Daughter. Rememeber me to your teachers and all the children. Good By from your loving Mother
Sarah Lunden

Hollidaysburg April 6th 1872
My Dear Little Jimmy,

I received your letter. When I opened it I wondered who it was from it was written so nicely. I turned it over and seen it was from my own little Jimmy. Such a nice long letter and so much in it and those pictures you draw, we all took a hearty laugh at them. And you are all glad to see Dr. Bourns when he visits the home. I don't wonder at it for you have such nice times when he is there. I should like to have seen the Girl's Fair and heard Ada's dialogue. I guess it was funny. I think you have every reason to like your teachers for they are very kind and good to you I know. Your little piece of poetry you write in your letter is very nice.

Hollidaysburg April 22nd 1872
My Dear Little Ada,

I received your letter and am sorry to keep you waiting so long but can not help it. I have been very buisy. I also received the 3 cards in your letter and three in Jimmy's. I will gather them up one

of these days and see how many you have sent me. Ada, I seen Carrie Clark on Saturday Evening and she told me she had commenced a letter to you. The man I told you had the small poxs he died. He didn't lay two weeks. He died on a Saturday morning and was buried in the afternoon. The Little Girl in the same house has it but she is getting well now. No Ada, none of us got It, we are all well. Georgie did like his teacher very much but there is no school now. It was stopped on account of the small pox. My Dear Little Daughter I know you and Jimmy are trying to be good children. I am proud of my two little darlings. You said you would send some things in your letter my Dear Little Girl. There was nothing at all in your letter but your cards. After I read the letter I looked on the floor but could find nothing. I suppose you did not put them in. Your Grandma Lunden was here a week ago. She is well and told me to tell you to write to her. She said she was going to write to you soon. Remember me to your teachers and all the children. I will close with lots of love to my Little Son and Daughter from your Loving Mother
    Sarah Lunden

Hollidaysburg April 29, 1872
    My Dear Little Jimmy,

    I have just set down tonight after a hard days sewing to answer your letter. It is too bad I kept you waiting so long and you would like Georgie to come to the Homestead. Jimmy, how could I spare him. I would be so lonely and he is such a good little boy. I think he will come sometime there. Now I have just taken him to bed he sends good night to brother and sister. You says you are going to have examinations. How I would like if I could just in to hear it but I can't and I want you and Ada to tell me all about it. Jimmy, I got Ada's cards but nothing more. I think she forgot to put them in the letter. Give my love to Katy Carter and all the rest of the children. Remember me to your teachers. It is bed time I must close my letter with much love to my little son and daughter. Good Night from your loving Mother.
    Sarah Lunden

Hollidaysburg May 21st 1872
    My Dear Little Son and Daughter,

    Jimmy I received your nice long letter. I am always so glad to hear from you and Ada. Give my love to Ella Frisbie and tell

her I took a good laugh over her dream about me. I don't know any of her friends you speak of. You have little gardens. I wish I could have sent you some flower seeds but it is most too late now. Grandma has hers all sown. Tell Ada I cannot send her those ear rings now. If she comes home this summer we will make it all right. I am going to send 50 cents in this letter 25 for each of you. I must close my letter now for I have to finish a pair of pants for tomorrow Dinner time I am very busy I can hardly get time to write. Give my love to all in the house and lots of love to my little Ada and Jimmy from you own loving Mother.
    Sarah Lunden

Holidaysburg June 24 1872
    My Dear Little Jimmy,
    I received your letter and ought to have answered it sooner but this is my buisy time. I still make Pantaloons for Mr. Goldman. He has so many to make I don't have time for anything else.
    Your Grandma Lunden was here on last Friday. She was well. I gave her your letter to read Your Aunt Lucy was here not long ago. She does not know now whether she will go to see you or not. Jimy you say you have a garden. I am pleased to know that my two little ones are so industrious it shows you want to work and be good. Ada and Jimmy Mother does love you so much. I do want to see you so bad but I can't come yet but you must still be looking out a place for me to stop at when I come. Tell me in your next letter how long vacation will last. I will come during vacation if I can get off. I would have sent you something with Mrs. Woods but I could not get out to Altoona to see her before she went. Georgie is well and sends love to brother and sister. I will close my letter for this time. Give love to all in the home with much Love I remain your affectionate Mother.
    Sarah Lunden

Homestead Orphange, Gettysburg PA July 23rd 1872
    My Dear Mother,
    I received your short letter telling me that you would come to see us as soon as you work done a little. We have not heard from you since you wrote to me a little sheet of paper. And Mrs. Woods wrote to Katie and told her that she had not heard from you nor seen you since she saw Katie and I am very anxious about you. The flowers in my garden are growing very nicely. I will send some

Georgie a fly and he must not let it bother him. The shew flys are very bad this time around here.

I will send you a little book Mr. Bourns gave me. Katie Carter is well and sends her best respects to you al. Jimmie and I are well and we hope you are well also. Good bye. Remember us dear Mother as ever your affectionate Daughter.

Ada Jane Lunden

Hollidaysburg July 1872

My Dear Little Ada,

I sit down to answer your letter. I am coming to see you as soon as I get through my work a little. I would have liked to you with Mrs. Woods but could not make it suit. Tell Mrs. Thorn I think she is a very kind. I will be very much obliged to her if she gets me a place to stop at. I will have a lot of pictures to show you when I come. I know you would be glad to see Mrs. Woods. She is so kind and so nice. I have not time to write much now. Give my love to all the little folks and your teachers and ever so much love for you and Jimmy. Good by from your own Loving mother.

Sarah Lunden

Drawing by Ada

Gettysburg Pa
Sept 4th 1872

My Dear Mother
            We have not received a letter ever since school commen I would like to hear from you very much.
        We are well and hope you are well also.
                Katie Baxter got a letter from her mother.
                I am very sorry you could not come any sooner for this month is quite cool.
    I will pack a nice little box for you when you come.
    The flowers in my garden are in bloom yet

I am studying history and warrens common school geography and spelling.

Jimmie is in the same class he was in before.

Tell grandma Lunden please to write to me as soon as she can.

Bella Hunter is well and sends her love to all of the family.

Mrs Harras and Mrs Richter will be here to night.

Mrs Carmichael and Mrs Brown took the children out to see Mr Weaver dig up the remains of the rebels.

The work I have got now is the little sewing room and I like it very much.

The boys keep chickens.

A balloon was going to go up on Saturday but the gas escaped.

This is all good bye from your loving Daughter, Ada Lunden

Homestead Orphanage, Gettysburg PA Sept 4th 1872

My Dear Mother,

We have not received a letter ever since school commenced. I would like to hear from you very much.

We are well and hope you are well also. Katie Carter got a letter from her mother.

I am very sorry you could not come any sooner for this month is quite cool. I will pack a nice little box for you when you come. The flowers in my garden are in bloom yet. I am studying history and common school geography and spelling.

Jimmie is in the same class he was in before. Tell Grandma Lunden please to write to me as soon as she can. Bella Hunter is well and sends her love to all the family. Mrs. Harris and Mrs. Reichter will be here tonight. Mrs. Carmichael and Mr. Bourn took the children out to see Mr. Weaver dig up the remains of the rebels.

The work I have got now is in the little sewing room and I like it very much.

The boys keep chickens.

A balloon was going to go up on Saturday but the gas escaped. This is all good bye from your loving Daughter, Ada Lunden

Homestead Orphanage, Gettysburg PA Oct 2nd 1872

My Dear Mama,

We have not received a letter from you since you left us and I would like to hear from you much. We are well and we hope you are well also. Jimmie could not write to you last week because he did not know the directions. All of the children are well. Baldwin is well and sends his love to you.

Jimmie told me to tell you he has not got that big slate pencil yet and that card Georgie gave him.

The girls are still playing with their dolls. Mama please tell Georgie we are waiting for him to come back again. When you write to me please send me the poetry you had put up in an envelope before you come to see us.

Mrs. Carmichael desires to be remembered to you and Georgie and she wants Georgie to come back.

From your affectionate daughter Ada J. Lunden

Gettysburg Pa
Oct 2nd 1872

My Dear Mama
We have not received a letter from you since you left us and I would like to hear from you much.
We are well and we hope you are well also.
Jimmie could not write to you last week because he did not know the directions.
All of the children are well.
Baldwin is well and sends his love to you.
I have not written to cousin Harry yet.
Jimmie told me to tell you he has got that big slate pencil yet and that card Georgie gave

him.

The girls are still playing with their dolls.

Mama please tell Georgie we are waiting for him to come back again.

When you write to me please send me the poetry you had put up in an envelope before you came to see us.

Mrs Carmichael desires to be remembered to you and Georgie & she wants Georgie to come back.

From you affectionate daughter Addah J Lunden.

Hollidaysburg, Noveber 3rd 1872
My two dear Little ones,
I received both your letters. I answer them now and send them with your Grandma who I know you will be glad to see. I will send Ada a pair of stockings and a pair of stockings for my little Jimmy too and I will send you each a sheet of paper and an envelope. Ada, your cousin Harry is waiting patiently on that letter we are going to write to him. You will in this letter find some poetry, the two pieces entitled Narrow Gauge and that Fine Fence. Give them to Baldwin with my Love. The Stocking Sermon is for Jimmy. Name in the Sand for Ada. I want you to learn them and tell me if you think they are nice. Jimmy tells me Ada made me one of her nice dresses it was a very pleasant surprise to me. I am very glad my little Girl can sew so nicely. Be good children and every body will love you. Give my love to Mrs. Carmichael and Etta and all the boys and girls. Remember me to Dr. Bourns. I will close my letter with lots of love for my little son and Daughter. Good by from your loving Mother. Sarah Lunden PS - Ada enclosed you will find 25 cents divide it between you and Jimmy

Homestead Orpphanage, Gettysburg, PA November 20th, 1872
My Dear Mother.
We received the things you sent us. We are both well. Also Mother please send me a pair of skate on Christmas. We are going to have a great time on Christmas. It is getting quite cold here. Addie and I are both well. This is all I have to say this time.
So good bye from your affectionate son, please write soon.
Jimmie Lunden

Hollidaysburg, December 25th, 1872
My Dear little Ada and Jimmy.
This is Christmas day. I wish you all a Merry Christmas and a happy New Year. Grandma is getting dinner ready while I am writing to you. I am going to send your box with this letter. I would have sent it on last Monday but I have been so busy that I could not get it ready. I will send you the two stockings you gave me when I was down to see you. The pink one is for Ada and the Blue one is for Jimmie. I also send you both a pair of gloves....
(NOTE: there is only one page of this letter...)

1873

Entrance of the Evergreen Cemetery, Gettysburg

In the fall of 1873, the initial rumors of mismanagement and neglect began due to the first death of an orphanage child. In September, a thirteen-year-old boy, Robert Turner of New York died of "inflammation of the bowels." No obituary appeared in the local newspaper. The child was buried by the GAR. Post # 9 on September 4, 1873 in Evergreen Cemetery. No permanent marker was erected. It is unknown if Dr. Bourns, as a physician, attended young Turner during his illness. [11]

Hollidaysburg, September 8th 1873
My Dear Little Children,
　　I received Ada's letter. I was very glad to hear from you it being the first since you left home. We are all well but Willy. He got burned real bad last Tuesday. He was melting brass in the foundry and made a miss step and fell down a pit there. And the pot of hot brass fell down on his back and it is very sore. The doctor comes to see him every day. It will be two or three weeks before he gets well. I know you will feel very sorry for him. Tell Jimmy, Georgie thanks him very much for what he sent him. He has not

fished any with the hook and line yet but he wears his Greely on his layback collar every Sunday to Sunday school. I think I have wrote you as long a letter as you wrote me. Tell my Little Jimmy to write to me when it comes his turn I will be looking for it. Remember me to Mrs. Carmichael and all the children. I will say good bye from your Loving Mother.
   Sarah Lunden

Hollidaysburg Oct. 13, 1873
   My Dear Little Children,
   I received your letter on Saturday Night after coming home from Uncle Franks. We are all very sad here and I know you and Jimmie will be very sorry to hear your Aunt Martha is dead. She died on the fourth of this month that was on last Saturday a week and we buried her on Monday the sixth. Your Little Cousins are left orphans as well as you are. Only they have lost a dear Mother as well. We all feel so sad. Your Aunt Sue is out at Uncle Franks and will stay with them awhile. Ada, you might wright to Aunt Sue and put a word in for your Little Cousins. Or write to Harry, he has been looking for a letter from you this is his address, Master Harry Henry, Henrietta, Pa. Give my love to Mrs. Carmichael and tell her she shall do with that black dress whatever she thinks. Remember me to all that are in the home. This little ribbon your Cousin Annie Henry sends you. With much love to Ada and Jimmy. Good night from your Loving Mother,
   Sarah Lunden

1874

Hollidaysburg Nov 12th 1874
   My Two Dear Little Boys,
   I thought I would write to you tonight. Why don't you write to me. I have not had a letter from Jimmie since I came home from the homestead. Oh, I do want to hear from you so bad. I had a letter from you Sister. It is most three weeks ago now. It is too bad that I can't hear oftener than that. I feel so lonely since Georgie is gone now. Jimmie I want you and Georgie to write a letter together to me and tell me everything about yourselves and your school. I know Mrs. Carmichael will let you if you ask her. Don't forget. I think sometimes I can't wait any long. That I must go right off to

see you. if I could hear from you oftener I wouldn't feel so bad. Jimmie I suppose you remembered the second day of this month was your birthday You was twelve years old. Jimmie, I gave Mr. Rollin the bullet you sent him. He was very much pleased to think you remembered so much. He took the bullet up to the desk in Sunday School and told the whole school where it came from and who sent it. And then he said if any of them wanted to see it they should come up to the desk after Sunday School was dismissed and look at it. Georgie, your Sunday School teacher has been inquiring about you. Georgie I just pulled your corn this evening. Our market basket is about half full. Grandma told me to tell

you she had some roasting ear of it but it wasn't very good to eat. Oh Georgie, your Aunt Mill has just come in and has brought me yours and Ada's letter. Oh, how glad I am to get them. If you knew how much good it does me to get your letters you would write oftener to me. Now I want to hear from my Little Jimmy. I want you and Georgie to write a letter together to you Mother and tell me what you are studying. Georgie this is only the second letter I have received from you since you have been at the homestead. Georgie. On Tuesday night there was a great time in town. The Democrats gained the election and they had a grand parade. They had banners and torches and men dressed up in rags. They had bundles on their backs and some had dresses on and false faces so that no one would know them. I tell you they looked gay. They said they was just coming down Salt River and the Republicans were going up. We all went out to see them. I think I have wrote you a long letter. Grandma and Aunt Mill sends love to you all. Give my love to Mrs. Carmichael, Etta and all the children and Lots of Love to Ada, Jimmie and Georgie

Your Mother, Sarah Lunden

The Gettysburg Homestead Orphanage

1875

It was in 1875 that reports of Rosa Carmichael's abuse truly began to circulate. On Christmas Eve, two men were walking home and passed the vicinity of the orphanage near midnight. They heard terrified shrieks on the bitterly cold night, and rushed to an outbuilding, which they discovered was the source of the "piteous screams." Breaking into the small outhouse, they found a four-year-old orphan boy, scantily clad in a thin nightshirt, who was "scared almost out of his senses." Mrs. Carmichael had locked the child inside as punishment for an infraction. Although this incident caused a public outcry, the investigation which had been made resulted in no actions being taken. Carmichael was allegedly able to find people who would lie for her, swearing false affidavits. Additionally, it is thought that children with marks and bruises were hidden until the inspections were ended.

Henrietta, February 18th, 1875

My Dear Little Children,

I thought I would write you a few lines. What in the world has come over you all. I have had no letters from either of you for going on two months. I can not think what is the reason. I wrote to you Ada and got no answer to it. I am here at Uncle Franks now. I have been here three weeks. Last Tuesday your Aunt Sue had a fell on the fore finger of her left hand...it has been very sore and I came out. Her finger is almost well now. She can work a little with it but she had an awful time poor Aunt Sue. She could not sleep at night for it pained her so bad. I am so glad it is better. So this is what I am doing here. Your Uncle Frank went over to Hallidaysburg last night and was at Grandmas and I told him if they had got any letters for me to send them with him to me and he came home today. Yet no letter. Well, Ada I was so disappointed I could have cryed. I just thought has my little children forgotten me or what is the matter? Now Ada I hope you will write to your own mother who thinks so much about you. If you would only write to me every two or three weeks I would be satisfied. But when you write, don't address it to Henrietta but to Hollidaysburg for I don't expect to be here much longer. Dear little ones I must close for your Cousin Molly is going to mail this for me now. Ada don't forget to write as soon as you get this. Lots of Love my Dear Little Children your Loving Mother,

Sarah Lunden

Hollidaysburg March 29th, 1875

My two Dear Little Boys,

I have not had a letter from either of you for oh so long. I want to hear from you so bad... can't you and Georgie write one a whole big sheet full. Tell me everything you know and you could write me a great big letter. Tell me something that will make me laugh for I get so lonesome and want to see you so bad. I think sometimes I can't wait any longer. If I could only walk there you would soon see your Mother coming up the pavement. I wonder if my little girl and boys would like to see me....

Aunt Mill sends love to Ada, Jimmy and Georgie and I will close with whole Lots of Love to my dear little children from your own Loving Mother.

Sarah Lunden

Good Night My Darlings

Hollidaysburg, April 15, 1875

My own Dear Little Daughter,

I received your very interesting letter and it was more interesting to me than any you have written since you have been in the Homestead. I am very much pleased with the presents you made for Mrs. Carmichael. I think it was so nice for you all to remember her on her birthday for she is so good and kind and I think she is given to her work. Not a bit too good for her and I know now all think that. Your Uncle Frank was here today and took your Grandma home with him and there is nobody at home now but your Aunt Mill and myself for Will is in Harrisburg. His brothers Dave and Frank were here on a visit and will had no work. So he thought it best to go with his brothers. They said he could get work there. Tell Georgie that Grandpapa was very much pleased with his letter and glad to hear from you all. Tell Jimmy and George I am waiting patiently for their letter. Tell them to write soon. Remember me to Mrs. Carmichael and all. Lots of love to my dear Little Jimmie and Georgie and the same to my Little Ada. From your Loving Mother

Sarah Lunden

"Home," June 18th 1875

My Dear Little Daughter,

I received your few lines with my Dear Little Jimmy's letter. Oh Ada you don't know how lonely and bad I feel when you don't write for so long. I wish you would write oftener. Say every two weeks. Well daughter, here is the dress you asked me for I have made it all but putting the band on the skirt and I think Ada can do that. I made it with a shirt waist. I expect it will be large for you but it is the best I could do. I made a belt of the same if it is too large you can let the hooks back on it. The reason I did not put the band on the skirt I was afraid of making it too short and I would like you to make it just to your shoe tops. Now Ada I want you to write after you have tried your dress on and tell me how it fits and how you like it. I hope it will please you. Ada tell Georgie I want him to write to me all about him. Tell Jimmy I will answer his letter before long. Oh, I want to see you so bad I hope it will not be long before I have that pleasure It is ten o'clock and Grandma is gone to bed. Aunt Mill is reading while I am writing to you. I think you are in

your little bed and may our good father watch over you all through this night is the prayer of your own Mother. Ada give lots of love to my dear little boys and a good share for yourself.
From Your Loving mother,
Sarah Lunden

Hollidaysburg, Sept 1st 1875
My Dear Little Children,

I guess you all wonder what has become of your mother. Well, Ada I was two weeks in Harrisburg with your Aunt Bell after I left you. She was sick and I staid till she was better and when I came home I found your photographs had got here before me. I think they are so good. I am very much pleased with Georgie's. Grandma and Aunt Mill thinks he has grown so tall they say it is so like him. Ada I gave one of yours and Jimmies to Hollie Garrett. She is going to get one taken especially for you but you must not look for it too soon but you will get it. Tell Georgie Aunt Mill thanks him very much for the present he sent her. She took a good laugh over it and she eat the raisin and currant for Georgie. And she sends this little comb for him. And tell him to let Jimmie use it too. Grandma sends love to all of you. She says she would just like to have Georgie to smooch and pinch tonight before she goes to bed. She is lonesome for somebody. She thinks it is Georgie. We have been cleaning house and I am very tired. I want you to write to me soon. Tell me all about yourself, Jimmy and Georgie. Give my love to Mrs. Carmichael and all the boys and girls. I will close with lots of Love to My Dear Little ones from you Mother
Sarah Lunden

1876

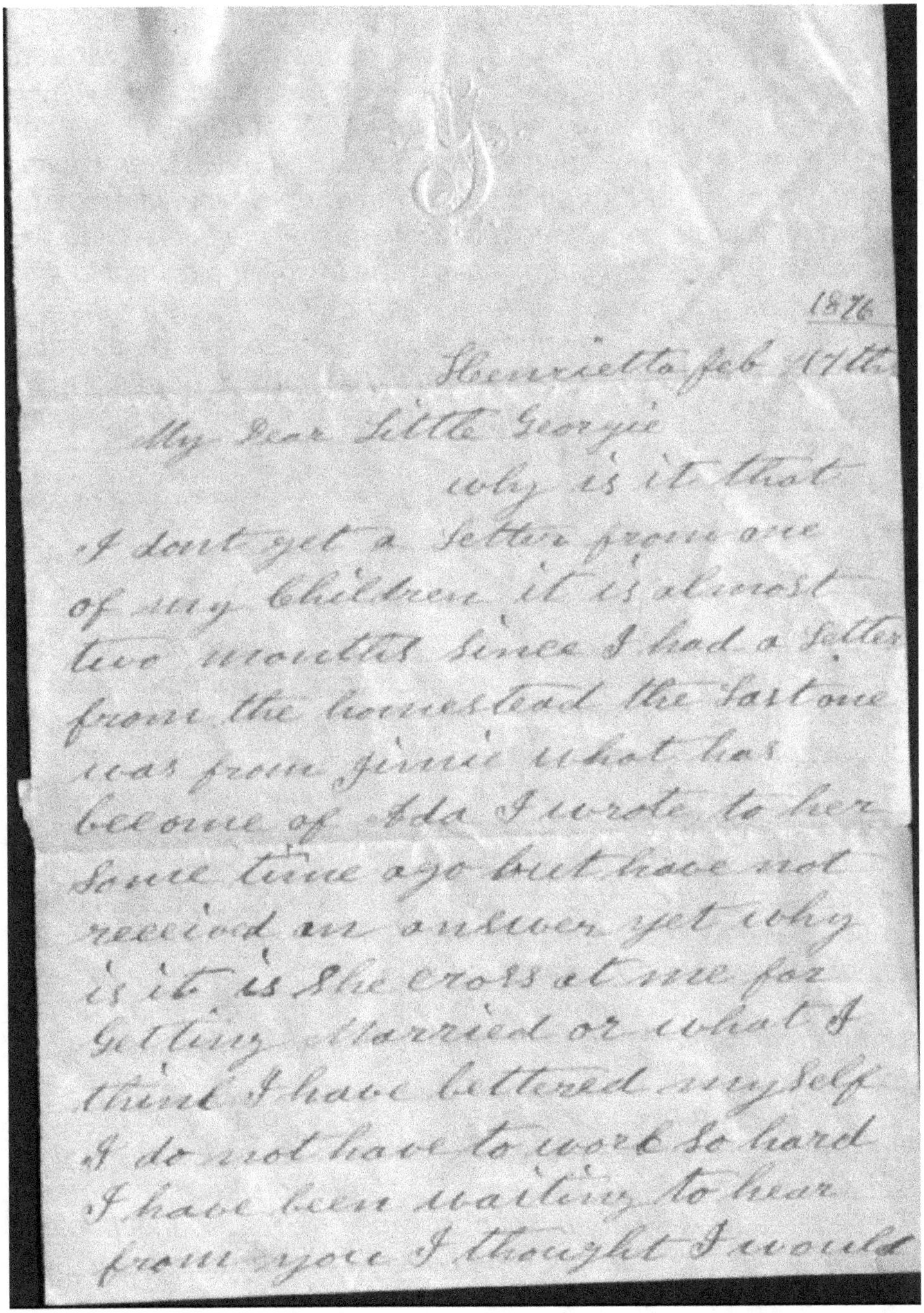

1876

Henrietta Feb 17th

My Dear Little Georgie

why is it that I dont get a letter from one of my Children it is almost two months since I had a letter from the homestead the last one was from Jimie what has become of Ada I wrote to her some time ago but have not received an answer yet why is it is she cross at me for getting Married or what I think I have bettered myself I do not have to work so hard I have been waiting to hear from you I thought I would

Henrietta, Feb 17th, 1876
My Dear Little Georgie,
Why is it that I don't get a letter from one of my children. It is almost two months since I had a letter from the Homestead. The last one was from Jimmie. What has become of Ada. I wrote to her some time ago but have not received an answer yet. Why is it? Is she cross at me for getting married. What I think I have bettered myself. I do not have to work so hard. I have been waiting to hear from you. I thought I would make up a nice little box for you now. Georgie do write to me soon and tell me every thing you know. Harry, Delia and Marcy have gone to spelling school tonight and there is no one up but Annie and myself. Uncle Frank and the little ones are in bed snoring away. Georgie tell Ada and Jimmie to write to me soon. If they don't I will get sick from my heart breaking. What I will close with. Lots of love to my own three little darlings from your own Mother.
Sarah Henry

Home, May 26th 1876
My Dear Little Ada and Jimmy,
Jimmy dear I guess you think I have forgotten you both but I have not. I have been very busy but I could think about you if I could not write. My Own Dear Little Jimmy, of course I forgive you for going away but have you asked God's forgiveness. Remember Jimmy, you have done wrong in his sight. I had a letter from Dr. Bourns stating your going away from the Homestead cost 20 twenty dollars. Just think of it Jimmy. Your Mother has that twenty Dollars to pay. But Mother forgives you and I hope you will never do so again. Next Sunday is the rededication of the church after being repaired. You remember it was all tore up when you and Ada was home last summer. We have had no preaching since. So it will be rededicated next Sunday. Tell Ada I was very glad to get my photograph back.
The hill in front of our house is getting so green and nice and the leaves are coming on the trees and everything looks so beautiful. Our cherry trees were very full of blossoms this summer and the pair tree to was very full of blossoms. I would so much to see you. I will close for this time with Lots of Love for Jimmy and Ada. Good by from your Mother
Sarah Lunden

Henrietta, July 27, 1876
My Dear Children,
Ada I received your letter some time ago and should have answered it sooner but have been very buisy and have had a great deal of company since I came home.

Well, Ada Dear this is your **sixteenth birthday**. When you write, tell me how many bumps you got. I will send you a little bouquet of flowers in this I will put sixteen in if I can. I got your pictures. I think they are very good. The girls are very much pleased with them and Frankie says it is splendid. When I came home Uncle Frank was in Altoona to meet me. And Mollie was in Hollidaysburg waiting for me. Your Cousin George Martin his wife and two children was here. They came in June was with us a couple of days then went to the centennial. Was there till after the fourth and came back and stayed a few days with us then left for home. Then Mrs. Garrett came out was with us a week and I had some nice drives we enjoyed theme. Ada tell Mrs. Carmichael I will come prepared to bring you home with me.

If I have to come and if not I will send for you. Ask her if she will please let me know when the time comes for I will not like to be at such expense for nothing. Mr. Henry thinks if they withdraw the suit that they would not be obliged to pay my expenses there and back. Ask her to please let me know all about it. I will close with Lots of love.
Your Own Mother,
Sarah Henry

This was the last letter from Sarah Lunden Henry to her children at the Homestead Orphanage. In the fall of 1876, charges of assault and the battery of George (Georgie) Lunden were brought against Rosa Carmichael. She called the charges "slanderous." However, Carmichael was found guilty and charged $20 plus "the cost of her arrest." Unbelievably, she was allowed to return to the Homestead and resume her position as headmistress. [12]

Ada Lunden moved to Hollidaysburg and continued to correspond with her fellow "inmates" many years later. The following two letters from Sadie Farley include noteworthy mentions of both Dr. Bourns and Rosa Carmichael.

Philadelphia, May 10, 1887 – From Sadie Farley to Ada Lunden[13]

Dear Ada,

I have just finished a letter to a friend of mine in Boston and will now answer your letter. It is just eleven years today since the Centennial Exhibition. How time does fly? Do you remember how Dr. Bourns used to tell us children at Gettysburg how he would bring us all down to see the exhibition. I remember so well how I used to look forward to it. How many promises Dr. B. made to us children that were never realized. I see Dr. B. once in awhile. He is getting very old and feeble. He called at the store one day to see me. I did not treat him very cordially nor encouraged to come again. He caused mother very much trouble. She had to resort to law to get us away from Gettysburg and he acted very meanly by her. I wonder what has become of Mrs. Carmichael. She was a bad woman, unfit to take charge and have control over children.

I want so badly to come to Hollidaysburg this summer. I do want to have a good talk (writing is so unsatisfactory.) with you about old times. I will not give up the hope of seeing you.

How I do associate the children with their numbers. You, 78 Jimmie 52, Eddie 33, Angie 103, Millie 105, Frank Humiston, 21, Sammy Dickson as we called him then, 23. I believe I can remember them all. Often when I want to remember a number, I will say that was "so and so" at Gettysburg.

When you write to Angie, give my love and best wishes for her future welfare. I wonder if she will remember Sadie Farley.

I must close now as it is getting late. Excuse all the scribbling and mistakes.

Remember me to Jimmie. Hope to hear from you very soon. I am you loving friend.

Sadie Farley

her. I wonder what has become of Mrs. Carmichael? She was a bad woman, unfit to take charge and have control over children.

I want so badly to come to Hollidaysburg this summer. I do want to have a good talk (writing is so unsatisfactory) with you about old times. I will not give up the hope of yet seeing you.

How I do associate the children with their numbers. You 78, Jimmie 52, Eddie 33, Angie 103, Millie 105, Frank Humiston, 21

Chester Street, Philadelphia, 1889

Philadelphia June 9, 1889 – From Sadie Farley to Ada **Lunden**[14]

Dear Ada,

How warm it has been today. I am afraid we are going to have summer in earnest now. I received a letter from Brother today. He desired to be remembered to you & asked your address. He said, "I might take it into my head to write to her." I will be surprised if he does. He can not bear to write and his letters to me are very few and far between.

Indeed, I do remember the Decoration days at Gettysburg. They, and the Fourth of July and Christmas were our Red Letter Days. To this day I remember some of hymns or songs rather, that we sang in the Cemetery. I should love to visit Gettysburg. I wonder if Uncle John is living yet. You ask me when I intend taking my vacation. I should like to have it within the second and third weeks of August or the third and fourth. If I can not have these I will wait until September rather than take it in July.

I saw Dr. Bourns on Chestnut Street last evening. I was so afraid he would recognize me and speak to me that I hurried past. He did not seem very much changed. Only that his face was very red and his eyes were bleared looking. I wonder whether he drinks. I hope not. Have you heard anything of his brother?

Decoration Day

He use to write to us, but somehow or other the correspondence ceased and we have not heard anything from him for years. I do want to come this summer and if possible I will. Write very soon. Remember me to Jimmie.
    Lovingly your friend,
    Sadie Farley

Relations became increasingly strained between Rosa Carmichael and the local chapter of the Grand Army of the Republic. Ever since 1868 and the proclamation of the first Decoration by the national head of the GAR, the children of the Homestead had led the procession to the recently dedicated Soldiers' National Cemetery to strew flowers on the graves of the honored veterans.

But in 1876, the GAR took charge of the annual ceremony. This seems to have angered Mrs. Carmichael. She forbid the Homestead orphans to participate in the observance. From the windows of the Homestead, the orphans had to watch others taking their place in the march to the cemetery. The GAR began an investigation shortly after Carmichael refused to allow the orphans to participate in the annual Memorial Day procession.

Two members of the state department of the GAR journeyed to Gettysburg and investigated rumors of neglect at the Homestead. They found that the institution was $2,000 in debt and only 30 orphans remained: "We have been forced to the conclusion that the institution has outlived its usefulness. Its revenues are small and unreliable, its indebtedness large and daily growing, its number of pupils small and sundry alleged claims against it large." The later reference was to the rumors circulating in the town about the conduct of Mrs. Carmichael. The two GAR men recommended "the closing of the Homestead at once and the transfer of the children to their respective homes or such charitable institutions as may be decided by the Board." A local attorney should be employed to replace Mrs. Carmichael and settle any claims against it. [15]

But nothing happened until the Assistant Adjutant General of the state GAR, Captain John M. Vanderslice of Philadelphia, arrived in Gettysburg for the festivities of Decoration Day in 1877. On his return to Philadelphia he published a report about all the stories and rumors that he had heard at Gettysburg. His story soon appeared in the local Gettysburg newspapers. The community was now aroused. What had formerly been only rumor was out in the open. He charged Dr. Bourns with exerting a dictatorial control over the orphanage, disregarding the wishes of the Board of Directors. He claimed that Mrs. Carmichael was "evil" and that none of the children had attended school for two years.

Vanderslice then listed several examples of Mrs. Carmichael's abuses:

"She employed a vicious boy, 19 years old and a former Homestead orphan to beat and kick "in a most cruel manner little children of a tender age and does it to the apparent delight of the matron and her certain approval." This boy became known as "Stick Boy," in lore due to his penchant of always carrying a beating stick.

A little girl was forced to stand on top of a school desk until "she was lifted down exhausted and helpless."

Other girls were forced to wear boy's clothing. Young Bella Hunter, (Ada's friend and bedfellow) age 17 and formerly "bright eyed," was now a "miserable, broken-spirited girl" and "the slave of Mrs. Carmichael." She had to perform the "most menial tasks, was locked in her room the rest of the time [and was] beaten and kicked." According to the GAR Captain the people of Gettysburg knew of poor Bella's misery but "there was none, it would seem, to intercede for her."

"These are just a few of the abuses and cruelties practiced in the place," thundered Captain Vanderslice. "Are they to be allowed to continue? Should the evil Mrs. Carmichael be allowed to remain? Should Bourns continue to use the orphanage as "a summer home waited upon by the little inmates, while their fathers sleep in the adjoining cemetery? Would the Board of Directors take any action? Must it be left to the Grand army of the Republic to intercede in behalf of the hapless inmates and abolish this nuisance." [16]

In the meantime, more shocking stories made the rounds in Gettysburg. Children supposedly had been suspended in barrels of bitterly cold well water by their arms. A deep dungeon existed in the cellar of the Homestead, a black hole 8 feet long, 5 feet deep and 4 feet wide. Here, the children who were considered "incorrigible" were shackled to the wall in utter darkness with practically no ventilation. There was no age limit for this punishment, children as young as four and five years old were allegedly shackled and suspended in the "dungeon" for days at a time.

A modern photograph of the Basement of the Homestead, with replica shackles

In June 1877, a young man escaped from the Homestead and made his way to Waynesboro, where he reported the actions of his notorious headmistress to the townspeople.

The Waynesboro Record printed the accusations: "A youth, about 19 years of age, who gave his name as Richard Hutchinson, who had part of his left arm off, passed through our town the other day. He said he came from the Orphan's Homestead at Gettysburg, and he made some statement in reference to the treatment of orphans there, which, if correct, would seem to show that the Home in question is no credit either to Gettysburg or to whoever manages it."

The charges were investigated and found to be true. The children were shoeless, malnourished and in rags. A reporter from the Gettysburg Star and Sentinel wrote: "She (Carmichael) has gone from bad to worse until the institution has become a public disgrace beyond the tolerance of decent people."

Mrs. Carmichael was again arrested and soon left town, never to be seen again. Dr. Burrowes was charged with embezzlement - "mismanagement, waste of property and the violation of trust."

But he never went to trial. In December 1877 the last orphans were taken out of the Homestead. Three orphans were adopted, three were sent to live with distant relatives, and three were sent to the "Home of the Friendless," the orphanage that Mr. and Mrs. Hutter had founded in Philadelphia.

Shackles used by Mrs. Carmichael at the "Soldiers Orphans' Homestead" Gettysburg Pa.

The Homestead property was sold at a Sheriff's sale during the summer of 1878. The household goods were sold at a public auction. The local GAR post bought a pair of iron shackles said to have been used by Carmichael. A photographer made an image of the shackles, providing a photographic coda to a story that started because of another photograph.¹⁷

Dr. Bourns resumed his medical practice and died in 1899.

Was he a benevolent patron or a financial crook?

Years later the enigmatic man composed a poem, "Left Alone:"

> *Thou Light alone the powers of*
> *Darkness come,*
> *Environing where thou has ever shone;*
> *Hope and perception grope in baffling gloom;*
> *Despair's chill terror in my soul I own,*
> *And hope abandoned, no I am alone* ¹⁸

CLIFF ARQUETTE'S — SOLDIERS MUSEUM

The actual buildings of the old Homestead have survived into modern times. For many years both buildings were private residences. Eventually, the girl's residence became a bed and breakfast. The boy's dormitory was purchased in the 1950's by a TV celebrity, Cliff Arquette alias Charlie Weaver, and turned into a military museum, The Soldiers' National Museum. After Weaver, a number of owners continued the museum which housed "genuine, restored and reproduced headgear, medals, and weapons." Its chief attraction was a visit to Mrs. Carmichael's infamous underground dungeon. It finally closed in 2014.

Modern Day replica of "the dungeon" complete with child mannequin

But all is not forgotten. Amazingly, the place is unlocked on designated evenings and guides take visitors on a tour of the underground dungeon for around $15.00 per person. These nocturnal excursions are particularly popular with "paranormals," and "ghost hunters," who claim that they can hear the cries of the abused orphans and the gloating of Rosa Carmichael, along with apparitions of those who were good and those who were evil.

END NOTES

CHAPTER ONE

[1] Sylvester Stevens, "Pennsylvania," 203

[2] Robert Bremner, "American Philanthropy," 70; Emerson Fife, "Social and Industrial Conditions During The Civil War," 287-289

[3] "Seventh Annual Report of the Northern Home," 4; James L. Paul, "Soldiers' Orphans Schools of Pennsylvania," 169-517 (hereafter cited as Paul, S.O.S.) ; Board of Public Charities of Pennsylvania, 1873, 44-97

[4] U.S. Bureau of the Census, 1860, 22

[5] Thomas H. Yundt, "A History of the Bethany Orphans' Home," 37

[6] Paul, S.O.S., 368, 516.

[7] Paul, S.O.S., 376, 426, 447

[8] Dudley Miles, "Photographic History of the Civil War," 146

[9] "Thirteenth Annual Report of the Northern Home," 6

[10] Philadelphia Inquirer, December 4, 1863.

[11] James Wickersham, "A History of Education in Pennsylvania," 587.

[12] Philadelphia Inquirer, December 4, 1863; Pages 3 – 7 : Samuel P. Bates, "Martial Deeds of Pennsylvania," 965-966.

[13] Legislative Record of Pennsylvania, 1864,15

[14] James Wickersham, "Report of the Superintendent, Annual Report of the Soldiers' Orphan, 1871" (hereafter cited as Annual Report, S.O.S., 1871), 307

[15] Legislative Record, 1866, 567; Pennsylvania School Journal, XVI, 1867, 231.

[16] Bates, "Martial Deeds," 965.

[17] Harrisburg Patriot, September 12, 1861.

[18] Stanton Davis, "Pennsylvania Politics, 1860-1863," 305

[19] Franklin (County) Depository, September 30, 1863

20 York Democrat Gazette, August 18, 1863.

21 Davis, "Pennsylvania Politics," 209.

22 Rebecca Albright, "Civil War Career of Andrew Gregg Curtin," Eastern Pennsylvania Historical Magazine, April, 1965, 160.

23 ibid., October 1964, 329; Thomas A. Scott to Andrew Gregg Curtin, December 23, 1862, Meredith Papers, Historical Society of Pennsylvania; Legislative Record, 1863, 12.

24 Albright, "Civil War Career," 370, 113, 182,

25 Stevens, "Pennsylvania," 204; Pages 7 – 8: Wayland Dunaway, History of Pennsylvania, 416.

26 Stevens, "Pennsylvania," 204

27 Dunaway, "History of Pennsylvania," 423.

28 Bates, "Martial Deeds," 962; Sanford Higginbottom, "Pennsylvania and the Civil War," 61; William B. Hesseltine, "Lincoln and the War Governors," 344.

29 York True Democrat, July 12, 1865; E.J. Shimmel, "A History of Pennsylvania," 300.

30 . Pennsylvania School Journal, October, 1881, 161.

CHAPTER TWO

1. Judith Geisberg, "Orphans and Indians," 188.

2. The Daily Local (West Chester), February 18, 1889.

3. "Report of the Superintendent," Annual Report of the Soldiers' Orphan Schools of Pennsylvania, 1877, 1.

4. ibid., 1879, 1.

5. "Report of the Inspector," Annual Report of the Soldiers' Orphan Schools of Pennsylvania, 1879, 26-27.

6. "Report of the Female Inspector," Annual Report of the Soldiers' Orphan Schools of Pennsylvania, 1877, 67-68.

CHAPTER THREE

1. "Principal of the McAlisterville S.O.S." Legislative Record, 1866, 561;

1. "Principal of the Titusville S.O.S.," Annual Report of the S. O.S., 1871, 66.

2. Record Book C of the York Home, Box 69, York County Historical Society.

3. Pennsylvania School Journal, 1865, 127.

4. Pennsylvania School Journal, 1881, 45.

5. Record Book A of the York Home, Box 69, York County Historical Society.

6. Thomas Burrowes to Peter Willaimson, Nov 21, 1864, The McPherson Collection, Historical Society of Pennsylvania. Pages 21–23.

7. "Report of the McAlisterville Principal," Annual Report Of the Soldiers' Orphan Schools, 1865, 561.

8. Pennsylvania School Journal, 1865, 147.

9. Record Books A and C of the York Home, York County Historical Society.

10. "McAlisterville Principal," Legislative Record, 1866, 561.

11. "Report of Inspector Greer," Annual Report of the S.O.S., 1888, 40.

12. Record Book A of the York Home, Box 69, York County Historical Society.

13. Pennsylvania School Journal, 1867, 248.

14. "Report of the Superintendent," Annual Report of the S.O.S., 1864, 123.

15. Pennsylvania School Journal, 1873, 33.

16. "Report of the Superintendent," Annual Report of the S.O.S., 1884, vi.

17. Pennsylvania School Journal, 1870, 239.

18. "Report of the Superintendent," Annual Report of the S.O.S., 1872, 27-28.

19. Pennsylvania School Journal, 1881, 160.

20. "Report of the Superintendent," Annual Report of the S.O.S., 1872, xviii.

21. Ibid., 1872, 28.

22. "Report of the Female Inspector," Annual Report of the S.O.S. 1878, 31.

23. Paul, S.O.S. 46.

24. ibid., 159.

25. "Report of the Superintendent," Annual Report of the S.O.S., 1867, 23.

26. "Proceedings of the Third Annual Reunion of the S.O.S. Sixteeners of Pennsylvania, 1883," 4.

27. "Report of the Superintendent," Annual Report of the S.O.S., 1873, 27.

28. Pennsylvania School Journal, 1881, 160.

29. "Report of the Female Inspector," Annual Report of the S.O.S., 1872, 42.

30. "Report of the Superintendent," Annual Report of the S.O.S., 1874, 89-92.

31. Ibid., 1875, 90.

32. Legislative Record, 1874, 1262; ibid., 1875, 406, 1148; ibid., 1878, 975, 1930; ibid., 1883, 3313, 2802; Harrisburg Daily Patriot, May 23, 1883; Daily News (West Chester), February 15, 1883.

33. Legislative Record, 1881, 1475.

34. Lancaster Daily Express, July 25, 1872; Lancaster Daily Intelligencer, May 19, 1883; Shenango Valley News, June 22, 1882.

35. "Report of the Female Inspector," Annual Report of the S.O.S., 1871, 328.

36. "Report of the Superintendent,: Annual Report of the S.O.S., 1880, 31.

37. Ibid., 2.

38. Wickersham, History of Education of Pennsylvania, 596. 599.

39. Michael Katz, "The Irony of Early School Reform," 41.

40. Lawrence Cremin, Horace Mann, 100.

41. George Heiges, "The Mt. Joy Soldiers' Orphan School." Papers Read Before The Lancaster County Historical Society, 124.

42. Paul, S.O.S., 159.

CHAPTER FOUR

1. Pennsylvania School Journal, 1864, 13; ibid, 1865, 62, 185.

2. Pennsylvania School Journal, 1863, 176.

3. Paul, SO.S., 327.

4. Ibid., 466.

5. Ibid., 265.

6. "Report of the Superintendent," Annual Report of the S.O.S., 1866, 40.

7. Paul, S.O.S, 101, 155.

8. Harrisburg Telegraph, July 21, 1875.

9. "Report of the Superintendent," Annual Report of the S.O.S., 1866, 158.

10. Paul, S.O.S., 99.

11. Local News (West Chester), January 30, 1877.

12. Chester County Historical Society, HISTORY'S PEOPLE, 1.

13. Annual Report of the Superintendent of the Soldiers' Orphans, 1877, p14.

14. Maria Zankey, "Walking Through Yellow Springs History," West Chester Daily News, August 14, 2011. The newspaper writer quotes the description offered by the archivist of Historic Yellow Springs, Sandra Momyer

15. The West Chester Daily Local, July 7, 1922.

16. The Reading Eagle, August 16. 1922, page 6, "SIXTEENERS REUNION".

CHAPTER FIVE

1. "Report of the Uniontown Principal," Annual Report of the S.O.S., 1877, 155.

2. Ibid., 1879, 201.

3, Paul, S.O.S., 90-107.

4. "Report of the Superintendent," Annual Report of the S.O.S., 1872, 27; Higbee, "Rules and Regulations of the Soldiers' Orphan Schools," Pennsylvania School Journal, April, 1886, 415.

5. "Interview With Inspectress Attick," Pennsylvania School Journal, April, 1888, 418.

6. Inspector W.L. Baer, "U.S. History," Pennsylvania School Journal, April, 1866, 234.

7. James McFarland, "Speech to the PSEA Convention," Pennsylvania School Journal, September, 1864, 84.

8. "Report of Inspector Cornforth," Annual Report of the S.O.S., 1872, 34.

9. "Report of Superintendent McFarland," Annual Report of the S.O.S., 1867, 22.

10. "Report of Inspectress Hutter," Annual Report of the S.O.S., 1885, 19.

11. "Report of Superintendent Wickersham," Annual Report of the S.O.S., 1871, 86.

12. "Report of the Superintendent," Annual Report of the S.O.S., 1881, 22.

13. Ibid., 1880, 28.

14. Ibid., 1877, 47.

15. Ibid., 1880, 27.

16. Wickersham, "Editorial," Pennsylvania School Journal, March 1874, 280.

17. James Mulhern, History of Secondary Education in Pennsylvania, 527.

18. "Report of Superintendent Burrowes," Annual Report Of the S.O.S., 1866, 158.

19. Paul, S.O.S., 140.

20. "Report of the Principal of the Chester Springs S.O.S.," Annual Report of the S.O.S., 1887, 78.

21. " Report of Superintendent Wickersham," Annual Report of the S.O.S., 1871, 87.

22. Pennsylvania School Journal, 1865, 77.

23. "Report of the Superintendent," Annual Report of the S.O.S., 1866, 103-106.

24. George Heiges, "The Mt. Joy S.O.S.," Paper Read Before the Lancaster County Historical Society, 1944, 118-119.

25. The Jeffersonian (West Chester). April 18, 1868.

26. George Heiges, ibid., 124.

27. Maria Zankey, "Walking Through Yellow Springs History," West Chester Daily News, August 14, 2011. The newspaper writer quotes the description offered by the archivist of Historic Yellow Springs, Sandra Momyer.

28. Paul, S.O.S., 101.

29. Ibid., 102.

30. Daily Local News (West Chester), April 16, 1888.

31. Daily Local News (West Chester). April 13, 1888.

32. Pennsylvania School Journal, 1866, 85.

33. "Report of Inspectress Attick," Annual Report of the S.O.S., 1888, 5.

34. ibid., 12.

35. "Principal of the Phillipsburg S.O.S." Annual Report of the S.O.S., 1876, 57.

36. "Principal of the Mercer S.O.S.," Annual Report of the S.O.S., 1878, 50.

37. "Principal of the Phillipsburg S.O.S.," Annual Report of the S.O.S., 1876, 29.

38. The Daily Local(West Chester), May 8, 1889.

39. The Daily Local (West Chester), May 12, 1886.

40. Ibid., May 1, 1886.

41. Ibid., September 18, 1888.

42. Ibid., September 29, 1890.

43. Ibid., March 10, 1876.

44. Report of the Commission of the S.O.S., 1893, 23.

45. Maria Zankey, "Walking Through Yellow Springs History," West Chester Daily News, August 14, 2011. The newspaper writer quotes the description offered by the archivist of Historic Yellow Springs, Sandra Momyer.

46. "Report of Superintendent Higbee," Annual Report of the S.O.S., 1888, 77, 103.

47. The Daily Local (West Chester), July 15, 1873; September 12, 1873; November 21, 1873; January 12, 1874; April 16, 1874.

48. Philadelphia Inquirer, March 16, 1865; Pennsylvania School Journal, July 1865, 230.

49. Pennsylvania School Journal, August, 1886, 36. Pages 75–82.

50. Judith Geisberg, "Orphans and Indians", 196.

51. Mt Joy Star, July 6, 1876.

52. George Heiges, "The Mt. Joy Soldiers' Orphan School,"Paper Read Before the Lancaster County Historical Society, 1944, 119.

53. The Times of Philadelphia, May 28, 1888.

54. "Report of the Superintendent," Annual Report of the S.O.S. 1885, 92.

55. George Heiges, "The Mt. Joy S.O.S.," Paper Read before the The Histroical Society of Lancaster County, 1944, 123.

56. Ibid., 123.

57. The Daily Local (West Chester), April 29, 1886.

58. Maria Zankey, "Walking Through Yellow Springs History," West Chester Daily News, August 14, 2011. The newspaper writer quotes the description offered by the archivist of Historic Yellow Springs, Sandra Momyer.

59. "Report of the Superintendent," Annual Report of the S.O.S., 1885, 92.

60. Paul, S.O.S., 154.

CHAPTER SIX

1. Pennsylvania School Journal, 1867, 89.

2. Armour, Lives of the Governors, 462.

3. Legislative Record of Pennsylvania, 1878, 1930.

4. Ibid., 1881, 1474.

5. Ibid., 1883, 2802.

6. Carlisle Herald, July 24, 1879; Mt. Joy Star, July 29, 1875.

7. Harrisburg Telegraph, July 12, 1872.

8. Paul, S.O.S., 132; "Report of Inspector Cornforth," Annual Report of the S.O.S., 1872, 32.

9. Philadelphia Record, February 22, 1886.

10. Harrisburg Daily Patriot, Lancaster Daily Intelligencer, Philadelphia Times, Harrisburg Telegraph, Wellsboro Agitator, February 23, 1886; Philadelphia Press, March 13, 1886; Connellsville Courier, March 26, 1886.

11. Philadelphia Record, march 13, 1886; "'Resolution of March 2, 1886," Minuite Book of GAR Post 33, Philadelphia, Pennsylvania.

12. Grand Army of the Republic, Department of Pennsylvania, Proceedings of the Annual Encampment, 1886, 4 (hereafter referred to as the GAR); Harrisburg Daily Patriot, February 25, 1886.

13. Harrisburg Daily Patriot, February 25, 1886.

14. New York Daily Tribune, April 16, 1886; New York Times, March 7, 15, 17, 1886.

15. Robert E.Pattison to Lewis Cassidy, April 15, 1886 quoted in the Harrisburg Daily Patriot, April 16, 1886.

16. GAR, 1887, 13.

17. GAR, 1888, 281.

18. GAR, 1889, 238.

19. Annual Report of the S.O.S., 1889, 92-95; Legislative Record, 1889, 273, 1234-1235, 2162, 2187.

20. Philadelpha Record, July 30, 1889; Harrisburg Daily Telegraph, July 30, 1889; Philadelphia Public Daily Ledger, July 31, 1889; Lancaster Daily Intelligencer, July 30, 1889.

CHAPTER SEVEN

1. Annual Report of the S.O.S., 1864, 178.

2. Pennsylvania School Journal, September, 1873, 51.

3. Annual Report of the S.O.S., 1885, 33.

4. Pennsylvania School Journal, September, 1873, 51.

5. Annual Report of the Northern Home, 1883, 15, 17; "Report of Inspectress Hutter,," Annual Report of the S.O.S., 1880, 31; ibid., 1884, 20; ibid., 1885, 19.

6. Annual Report of the Northern Home, 1883, 15.

7. Annual Report of the S.O.S., 1878, 31.

8. Pennsylvania School Journal, February 1870, 278.

9. Pennsylvania School Journal, September, 1873, 51.

10. Annual Report of the SOS 1864, 278.

11. "Act of 1876" Annual Report of the SOS, 1889, 88.

12. "Report of Superintendent James McFarland.," Annual Report of the SOS 1869, 38.

13. Annual Report of the SOS , 1867.21 Ibid, 21.

14. "Act of 1876" Annual Report of the SOS, 1889, 86.

15. "Principal of the Mansfield SOS," Annual Report of the SOS, 1886, 29, Paul SOS , 198.

16. Titusville Morning Herald, March 13, 1871.

17. "Report of the Inspector Cornforth," Annual Report of the SOS 1870 p 26, Ibid 1871, 341, Ibid, 1873, p 32, ibid 1874 p 34.

18. Annual Report of the SOS 1871, 383.

19. The Local News, West Chester, April 14, 1883.

20. "Principal of the Mercer SOS" Annual Report of the SOS 1873 Page 51: Ibid 1883, 33.

21. "Principal of the McAllisterville SOS, " Annual Report of the SOS 1871, 345.

22. Annual Report of the SOS, 1878 page 51.

23. Thomas Burrowes, "Speech to the PSEA Convention, 1869. Quoted in Mulhern, Secondary Education in Pennsylvania, 531.

24. Paul, SOS pg 90.

25. "Report of Inspector Greer," Annual Report of the SOS 1888, pg 66.

26. Mulhern, Secondary Education, 534.

27. Pennsylvania School Journal, September, 1867, 80.

28. Legislative record of Pennsylvania, 1889, 2565.

29. Lancaster Daily Express, July 19, 1873.

30. Annual Report of the S.O.S., 1873, 32.

31. Thomas Burrowes, "Speech to PSEA," Pennsylvania School Journal, September, 1867, 90.

32. "Report of the Mansfield S.O.S. Principal," Annual Report of the S.O.S., 1871, 344; ibid, 1878, 45.

33. "Report of the White Hall S.O.S. Principal," Annual Report of the S.O.S., 1887, 101.

34. "Report of the Mansfield S.O.S. Principal," Annual Report of the S.O.S., 1878, 45.

35. "Report of the Mansfield S.O.S. Principal," Annual Report of the S.O.S., 1871, 144; "Report of Inspector Cornforth," Annual Report of the S.O.S 1874, 34.

36. "Report of the White Hall S.O.S. Principal," Annual Report of the S.O.S., 1887, 101.

37. Annual Report of the S.O.S., 1888, 332.

38. Annual Report of the S.O.S., 1888, 332.

39. Harrisburg Daily Express, April 3, 1886; Governor Robert Pattison to Lewis Cassidy, April 15, 1886, quoted in Harrisburg Daily Patriot, April 16, 1886.

40. Legislative record of Pennsylvania, 1887, 3050, 3022, Pattison to Cassidy, April 15, 1886 quoted in Harrisburg Daily Patriot, April 16, 1886.

41. E.E. Higbee to Robert E. Pattison, April 23, 1886, quoted in The Pennsylvania School Journal, May, 1886, 455.

42. Journal of the Pennsylvania Senate, 1887, 88-89.

43. GAR, 1889, 238.

44. E.E. Higbee to Dr. Phillips, April 23, 1888, Chester County Historical Society.

45. GAR, 1892, 216.

46. Annual Report of the Commission of the S.O.S., 1892, 9, 10.

47. Ibid., 1906, 5.

CHAPTER EIGHT

1. Paul, S.O.S., 136.

2. Annual Report of the S.O.S., 1864, 772.

3. Paul, S.O.S., 189.

4. "Report of Superintendent Burrowes," Annual Report of the S.O.S., 1864, 780; "Report of the Principal of the S.O.S., Annual Report of the S.O.S., 1872, 46; James McFarland, "Soldiers' Orphan School," Pennsylvania School Journal, September, 18, 1867, 80.

5. ":Professor Fordyce A Allen," History of Tioga County, 899.

6. Philadelphia Record, march 23, 1886.

7. Annual Report of the S.O.S., 1875, 40.

8. Annual Report of the S.O.S., 1873, 4; ibid., 1877, 2;"Circular of Information," Pennsylvania School Journal, October, 1879, 159.

9. Pennsylvania Legislative Journal, 1871, 47.

10. Legislative Record of Pennsylvania, 1875, 2138.

11. Harrisburg Daily Patriot, May 23, 1883.

12. GAR. 1881, 63.

13. Lancaster Daily New Era, February 22, 1886; ibid., February 24, 1886; Connellsville Courier, March 26, 1886; Harrisburg Daily Patriot, March 24, 1886; Shenango Valley News, April 9, 1886.

14. Harrisburg Telegraph, march 20, 1886; Legislative Record, 1887, 3002; Samuel Skillen to Robert E. Pattison, March 11, 1886, Executive Correspondence of Governor Robert E. Pattison, Pennsylvania Historical Commission, Division of Public Records (hereafter cited as Pub Rec); Daily Local News (West Chester), March 4, 1886.

15. Harrisburg Daily Patriot, April 16, 1886; Dr. V.H Beachley to Robert E. Pattsion, March 10, 1886, Executive Correspondence, Pub Rec;

16. Carlisle American Volunteer, April 21, 1886.

17. Philadelphia Record, February 22, 1886; Melissa Wagner to Robert Pattison, March 12, 1886, Executive Correspondence, Pub Rec; Kittaning Times, March 26, 1886.

18. Harrisburg Telegraph, March 6, 1886; Kittaning Times, March 26, 1886.

19. Annual Report of the S.O.S., 1890, 2.

20. Pittsburgh Commercial Gazette, n.d., 1896 in scrapbook of the Scotland Industrial School.

21. Carlisle American Volunteer, March 3, 1886.

22. Legislative Record, 1887, 2938, 2972.

23. George W. Wright to J.P. Hipple, January 30, 1884, Legislative record, 1887, 3142.

24. Harrisburg Daily Telegraph, March 9, 1886; Pittsburgh Commercial Gazette, n.d., 1886, Scotland Scrapbook.

25. Pittsburgh Dispatch, March 8, 1886.

26. Harrisburg Daily Patriot, April 16, 1886.

27. Philadelphia Record, February 22, 1886.

28. Greenville Advance Argus, March 11, 1886.

29. Scranton Truth quoted in the Harrisburg Daily Patriot, March 13, 1886.

30. E.E. Higbee to Robert E. Pattison, March 6, 1886, Pennsylvania School Journal, April, 1886, 411.

31. Higbee, "The Orphan Schools," Pennsylvania School Journal, May, 1886, 444.

32. Harrisburg Daily Patriot, April 16, 1886; Philadelphia Record, February 22, 1886; Greenville Advance Argus, March 11, 1886.

33. Higbee, "The Orphan Schools," Pennsylvania School Journal, May, 1886. 444.

34. Greenville Advance Argus, March 4, 1886.

35. Legislative Record, 1889, 2565.

36. Philadelphia Public Ledger, March 9, 1886; Connellsville Courier, March 26, 1886.

37. Frank Leslie's Illustrated Weekly Newspaper, March 27. 1886; Harrisburg Daily Patriot, February 24, 1886; Robert E. Pattison to Lewis Cassidy, April 15, 1886 quoted in Harrisburg Daily Patriot, April 16, 1886; Philadelphia Record, April 17, 1886.

38. "Act of 1867," Annual Report of the S.O.S., 1889, 85, 97.. "Report of Inspectress Hutter," Annual Report of the S.O.S., 1870, 29; "Report of Inspector Cornforth," Annual Report of the S.O.S., 1869, 28.

39. Titusville Herald, July 10, 1884;

40. Altoona Tribune, August 16, 1883.

41. Legislative Record, 1870, 1927; ibid., 1881, 616; ibid., 1885, 604.

42. Legislative Record, 1887, 3158-3160.

43. "Report of Inspector Louis Wagner," Annual Report of the S.O.S., 1886, 52, 55-56, 58.

44. Legislative Record, 1887, 3699; Robert E. Pattison To Louis Cassidy, April 15, 1886, Williamsport Sun and Banner, n.d., 1886, Scotland Scrapbook.

45. Nathan Modrow to James Loar, n.d., quoted in the Legislative record, 1897, 3155; ibid., 1889, 2566; Ibid., 1887, 2926.

46. Legislative Record, 1887, 2926.

47. Robert E. Pattison to Lewis Cassidy, April 15, 1886, Harrisburg Daily Patriot, April 16, 1886.

48. Philadelphia Record, February 22, 1886; Harrisburg Daily Patriot, April 14, 1886.

49. Lancaster Daily New Era, February 24, 1886.

50. "Report of the Principal of the Dayton S.O.S.," Annual Report of the S.O.S., 1886, 72.

51. Greenville Advance Argus, March 5, 1886; Philadelphia Record, February 22, 1886; Philadelphia Public Ledger, February 25, 1886.

52. Lancaster Daily News, March 16, 1886; Philadelphia Press, March 13, 1886.

53. Philadelphia Record, February 22, 1886; Kittanting Times, March 15, 1886.

54. Harrisburg Daily Patriot, April 13, 1886; GAR, 1886, 12.

55. Greenville Advance Argus, March 4, 1886; Harrisburg Daily Telegraph, March 8, 1886.

56. M.S. McCullough to Mr. Darlington, May 11, 1870 Chester County Historical Society.

57. Lancaster New Era, February 26, 1886; Philadelphia Press, March 13, 1886.

58. Philadelphia Press, February 23, 1886.

59. Philadelphia Times, March 12, 1886; Harrisburg Telegraph, March 10, 1886; Connellsville March 26, 1886; Wellsboro Agitator, February 23, 1886.

60. Pottsville Miners Journal, February 26, 1886.

61. Pattison to Cassidy, April 15, 1886.

62. Legislative Record, 1887, 1896.

63. Pennsylvania School Journal, March 1887, 371.

64. GAR, 1887, 257; GAR, 1888, 255.

65. Amos Mylin, State Prisons, Hospitals, Soldier's Orphan Homes Controlled by the Commonwealth of Pennsylvania, 1897, 525.

66. Carlisle American Volunteer, March 6, 1886; Legislative Record, 1899, 1567; Daily Local News (West Chester), February 27, 1889. 130-135.

67. Legislative Record, 1889, 2563, 2567-2568.

68. Legislative Record, 1889, 1235, 2162, 2170.

69. Philadelphia Record, July 30, 1889; Harrisburg Telegraph, July 30, 1889.

CHAPTER NINE

1. Lancaster Daily Intelligencer, July 10, 1889.

2. Garrity, The New Commonwealth, 236-237; James Bryce, The American Commonwealth, 145, Evans, Pennsylvania Politics, 1, 7; Bradley, Militant Republicanism, 9; Dunaway, History of Pennsylvania, 438.

3. Evans, Pennsylvania Politics, 322, 8, 133; Bradley Militant Republicanism, 249, 357'; Stevens, Pennsylvania, 762, 773, 788.

4. Paul, S.O.S., 129.

5. Harrisburg Daily Patriot, March 10, 1886.

6. Wickersham, History of Education, 599.

7. James A McKee, History of Butler County, 1444.

8. Bradley, Militant Republicanism, 275; Burrowes, "Some Parting Thoughts," Pennsylvania School Journal, June, 1867, 301.

9. James P. Wickersham to W.A. Pennypacker, January 9, 1878, Chester County Historical Society.

10. Baer, Wickersham, 40; Eugene McCoy, "History And Development of the Pennsylvania Department of Public Instruction," (Univ of Pennsylvania Ph.D Thesis, 1959), 225.

11. Huntingdon Journal, February 18, 1874.

12. Huntingdon Monitor, March 30, 1874.

13. Stevens, Pennsylvania, 785-786; Lewis W. Rathberger, "The Democratic Party in Pennsylvania, 1880-1896," (Univ of Pittsburgh Ph.D Dissertation, 1955), 100.

14. Lancaster New Era, March 27, 1886.

15. Carlisle Herald, March 18, 1886; Chambersburg Repository, March 9, 1886.

16. Lancaster Daily New Era, March 16, 1886; Carlisle Herald, March 18, 1886; Carlisle American Volunteer, March 10, 31, 1886.

17. Dr. G.W. Yeager to Robert E. Pattison, February 26, 1886, Executive Correspondence, Pub Rec.

18. Samuel Skillen to Robert E. Pattison, March 11, 1886, Joseph Slosson to Robert E. Pattison, March 11, 1886, Executive Correspondence, Leg Rec.

19. Philadelphia Record, February 22, 1886.

20. Lancaster Daily Intelligencer, n.d 1886 in Scotland Scrapbook; Harrisburg Daily Patriot, March 16, April 16, 1886.

21. Philadelphia Record, February 22, 1886; Leg Rec, 1878 2390; Harrisburg Daily Patriot, March 11, 1886.

22. Pittsburgh Commercial Gazette, n.d. 1886 Scotland Scrapbook.

23. Harrisburg Daily Patriot, April 2, 1886.

24. Harrisburg Daily Telegraph, March 22, 1886.

25. Philadelphia Record, April 17, 1886 Harrisburg Daily Patriot, April 17, 1886 Pittsburgh Commercial Gazette n.d. 1886 Scotland Scrapbook.

26. Philadelphia Record, February 22 1886, Montrose Democrat March 12, 1886.

27. Philadelphia Record, February 22, 1886; Harrisburg Daily Patriot, Feb 24, March 10, April 16, 1886; Montrose Democrat, March 12, 1886.

28. Harrisburg Daily Patriot, April 25, 1886.

29. Bellefonte Democratic Watchman, n.d. , 1886 quoted in Harrisburg Daily Patriot, March 20, 1886.

30. Philadelphia Press, April 23, 1886.

31. Harrisburg Daily Telegraph, March 9, 1886.

32. Harrisburg Morning Call, March 11, 1886.

33. Harrisburg Daily Telegraph, March 10, 1886.

34. Harrisburg Morning Call, March 4, 1886; Greenville Advance Argus, March 4, March 15, 1886; Harrisburg Telegraph, February 25, 1886.

35. E.E. Higbee, "Honor of the State," Pennsylvania School Journal, March 1888, 334-335.

36. Pittsburgh Leader, March 19, 1886; Lancaster Daily new Era, March 23, 1886; Harrisburg Morning Call, March 22, 1886.

37. Carlisle American Volunteer, March 10, 1886.

38. Chambersburg Public Opinion, n.d., 1886 quoted Scotland Scrapbook.

39. Chambersburg Repository, March 2, 9, 13, 1886.

40. Harrisburg Daily Patriot, March 13, April 2, April 20, 1886.

41. Harrisburg Telegraph, April 13, 1886.

42. Harrisburg Daily Patriot, August 19, 1886; Carlisle American Volunteer, September 22, 1886.

43. Rathgeber, "Democratic Party," 154, 163.

44. Chauncey F. Black to the Nominating Committee of the Democratic State Convention, Sept 1886 quoted in York Democratic Press, Sept 24, 1886; York Democratic Press, October 29, 1886.

45. Harrisburg Daily Patriot, April 14, 1886; Philadelphia Press, April 13, 1886; Connellsville Courier, April 2, 1886.

46. E.E. Higbee, "Honor of the State," Pennsylvania School Journal, March 1888, 334.

47. Harrisburg Morning Call, March 11, 1886.

48. Harrisburg Daily Patriot, July 1, 1886.

49. Pennsylvania House Journal, 1887, 64.

50. Scranton Republican, n.d, 1886 quoted in Scotland Scrapbook.

51. Lancaster Daily New Era, July 10, 1889; Philadelphia Press, July 30, 1889.

52. Harrisburg Telegraph, July 10, 1889.

53. ibid., July 10, 1889.

54. Philadelphia Press, July 30, 1889; Daily Local News (West Chester), February 27, 1889.

CHAPTER TEN

1. Wickersham, History of Education in Pennsylvania, 587.

2. Pennsylvania School Journal, October, 1881, 162.

3. Harrisburg Telegraph, March 20, 1866.

4. Sixteeners' Association Proceedings, 1881, 5.

5. Wickersham, "A Word for Pennsylvania," Pennsylvania School Journal, November 1872, 159; Paul, SOS, 17. Annual statistics for the other states are not available but in those years checked, Pennsylvania did spend more money and aided more children than all of the other states combined. In 1878, the other states spent $142,700 for 1270 soldiers' orphans while Pennsylvania expended $172,748 on 2653 orphans. In 1883, the other states appropriated $254,800 for 1492 soldiers' orphans as compared to Pennsylvania's $352, 141 on 2306 children. Us Commissioner of Education, Report 1878, ibid, 1883, 711, 778.

6. Annual Report of the Pennsylvania SOS, 1889, 5.

7. Report of Inspector John Greer," Annual Report of the SOS, 1890, 45; Annual Report of the SOS 1889, 5: ibid, 1872, 30, ibid 1889, 5.

8. Thomas Burrowes to Henry Barnard, February 15, March 25, 1866 quoted in Mohr, Burrowes, 198.

9. Jennie Leonard, "Speech to PSEA Convention," Pennsylvania School Journal, May, 1865, 246.

10. James McFarland, "Speech at the PSEA Convention," Pennsylvania School Journal, September, 1871, 99.

11. James Wickersham, "Ungraded Schools," Pennsylvania School Journal May 1871, 17-20. In 1872, of the 16,800 schools in Pennsylvania only 4,500 were graded. Twenty years later ten thousand or still less than half of the twenty-three thousand common schools were graded. Report of the Superintendent of Public Instruction, 1872, v., ibid., 1890 vii.

12. Wellsboro Agitator, February 17, 1880.

13. U.S. Bureau of Education, Circular of Information, 1875, 417-418: Pennsylvania School Journal, September 1876, 126-127.

14. Wellsboro Agitator, February 17, 1880.

15. "PSEA Convention," Pennsylvania School Journal, September 1876, 126-127.

16. Legislative Record, 1885, 456-470, Legislative Record, 1887, 487-493, Legislative Record, 1895, 715-728, Legislative Record, 1874, 1469-1481.

17. Debates of the Convention to Amend the Constitutions of Pennsylvania, 1873, II, 446-449, 641-646:VI, 38-45, 61-85:VII, 682–695.

18. Report of the Superintendent of Public Instruction, 1886v-x; ibid, 1890, v;

ibid, 1891, v-ix.

[19.] Annual Report of the SOS, 1887, 3.

[20.] James Wickersham, "Our Neglected Children," Pennsylvania School Journal, August, 1883, 38.

[21.] First Annual Report of the Commission of Public Charities of Pennsylvania, 1871, iii.

[22.] James Wickersham, Report of the Superintendent of Public Instruction, 1871, xxiv; ibid, 1873, xxiii; 1880, xix-xx; ibid, 1871, xxiii.

[23.] Legislative Record, 1872, 1032.

[24.] Flynn, Public Care, 77.

[25.] Thomas Burrowes, "Soldiers' Orphans," Pennsylvania School Journal, May, 1865, 245.

[26.] Ibid., 245.

[27.] Rutherford B. Hayes, "Speech at Dayton, Ohio, July 13, 1869, quoted in Hughes and McCracken, The History of the Ohio Soldiers' and Sailors' Orphan Home 37, 7.

[28.] Report of the U.S. Commissioner of Education, 1883, 771, 778.

[29.] Davie, "Patriotism On Parade", 144.

[30.] Michael Dreese, "An Imperishable Fame", 9.

[31.] "Speech of Governor Curtin to the Legislature," March 16, 1866, quoted in Paul, SOS, 74-75.

THE Ill-FATED GETTYSBURG ORPHANAGE

[1.] "Philadelphia Inquirer" October 19, 1863.

[2.] Dunkelman, Mark, "Gettysburg's Unknown Soldier", pg 150.

[3.] Ibid pg 173.

[4.] Collins, Mary Ruth, "One Sodiers's Legacy", pg 29-30.

[5.] Ibid. pg 25.

[6.] 'The Gettysburg Compiler", July 1, 1870.

[7.] Ibid pg 155.

[8.] Dunkelman, Mark, "Gettysburg's Unknown Soldier", pg 199.

9. Ibid pg 199.

10. Wade Hall Collection of American Letters, Ada Jane Lunden Papers Series, 1870-1888 (bulk dates 1870-1876)

11. Collins, Mary Ruth "One Sodiers's Legacy", pg 59.

12. The Gettysburg Experience, May 2014.

13. Wade Hall Collection of American Letters, Ada Jane Lunden Papers Series, 1870-1888.

14. Ibid.

15. Dunkelman, Mark, "Gettysburg's Unknown Soldier", pg 202.

16. Ibid pg 204.

17. Zeller, Bob, "The Blue and Grey in Black and White," pg 188.

18. Dunkelman, Mark, "Gettysburg's Unknown Soldier," pg 209.

SELECT BIBLIOGRAPHY

Manuscript & Letter Collections

Chester County Historical Society, Letter Collection
Historical Society of Pennsylvania, MacPhearson Collection
Historical Society of Pennsylvania, Meredith Papers
Historical Society of Pennsylvania, Simon Grats Collection
Historical Society of Pennsylvania, Peter Williamson Collection
 Loyal Legion of Philadelphia, Minute Book of the Col. James Ashworth Post, No. 334, Department of Pennsylvania, Grand Army of the Republic
 Pennsylvania Historical and Museum Commission, Records of the Commonwealth of Pennsylvania, Executive Correspondence, 1861- 1891
 Susquehanna County Historical Society, Letter Collection.
 Wade Hall Collection of American Letters, Ada Jane Lunden Paper Series, 1870-1888 (bulk dates 1870 – 1876) University of Kentucky Library Archives.
 York County Historical Society, Manuscript Box 71. Record Books of the Children's Home of York, Pennsylvania, 1865 – 1880

Public Documents

Annual Report of the State Board of Charities of Pennsylvania, 1870-1875
 Annual Report of the Superintendent of the Common Schools of the Commonwealth of Pennsylvania, 1865 – 1874
 Annual Report of the Superintendent of the Public Instruction of the Commonwealth of Pennsylvania, 1875-1890
 Annual Report of the Superintendent of the Soldiers' Orphans of Pennsylvania, 1864-1889
 Annual Report of the Pennsylvania Commission of Soldiers' Orphan Schools, 1890 – 1900
 Debates of the Convention to Amend the Constitution of Pennsylvania. 1773, Volume II, VI, VII.
 Journal of the House of Representatives of the Commonwealth of Pennsylvania, 1861 – 1895.
 Journal of the Senate of the Commonwealth of Pennsylvania, 1861-1895.
 The Legislative Record, Containing the Debate and Proceedings of the Legislature of Pennsylvania, 1861 – 1895.
 Reed, George E., ed., *Papers of the Governors*. 1861- 1902 in Pennsylvania Archives,

Fourth Series, 1902.

United States Bureau of Education, *Annual Report, Circular of Information, No. 6, 1875.*

United States Commissioner of Education, *Annual Report*, 1870-1886.

United States Bureau of the Census, *Historical Statistics of the United States*, 1960.

United States Bureau of the Census, *Preliminary Report of the Eighth Census*, 1860.

REPORTS

Annual Report of the Children's Home for the Borough and County of York, 1872-1880

Annual Report of the Northern Home for Friendless Children, Philadelphia, Pennsylvania, 1854-1883

Grand Army of the Republic, Department of Pennsylvania, Proceedings of the Annual Encampment, 1867-1895

Proceedings of the First Annual Reunion of the Graduates of the Soldiers' Orphan Schools of Pennsylvania, 1881.

Proceedings of the Annual Reunion of the Soldiers' Orphan Sixteeners of Pennsylvania, 1882, 1883

NEWSPAPERS AND PERIODICALS

Altoona:
Morning Tribune, 1883.
Beaver:
Argus. 1866, 1871 – 1876.
Bloomsbury:
Columbia Democrat, 1865-1868.
Carlisle:
American Volunteer, 1885-1890
Herald, 1871-1874, 1877-1890
Chambersburg:
Franklin Repository, 1861-1865.
Repository, 1886.
Chester:
The Jeffersonian, 1868-1871.
West Chester Daily Local News, 1871-1890.
Connelleville:
Courier, 1879-1890.
Greenville:
Advance Argus. 1871-1890.

Shenango Valley News. 1882-1890.
Harrisburg:
Daily Patriot. 1863-1893.
Daily Telegraph. 1863-1891.
Morning Call. 1871-1890.
Pennsylvania School Journal. 1862-1896.
Huntingdon:
Globe: 1870-1874.
Journal: 1871-1874.
Monitor. 1870-1874.
Kittanning:
Times. 1876-1891.
Lancaster:
Daily Express. 1866-1875.
Daily Intelligencer. 1877-1893.
Daily New Era. 1877-1893.
Liverpool, Pennsylvania:
Sun, 1882-1889.
Mansfield:
Advertiser, 1872-1890
Montrose:
Democrat, 1870-1890.
Independent Republican,1865.
Mount Joy:
Star, 1875-1876.
New York:
Frank Leslie's Illustrated Newspaper, 1886.
Harper's Weekly, 1863.
Times, 1886.
Tribune, 1886.
Norristown:
Daily Herald. 188-1889
Philadelphia:
Daily Times. 1870-1890.
Inquirer. 1860-1893.
Press. 1879-1890.
Public Ledger. 1886.
Record. 1885-1890.
Pittsburgh:
Dispatch. 1886.
Leader. 1886.
Pottsville:

Miners Journal. 1871-1889.
Reading:
Eagle. 1884.
Scotland Soldiers' Orphan School:
Industrial school News. 1896-1898
Titusville:
Morning Herald. 1867-1875.
Wellsboro:
Agitator. 1867-1886.
York:
Democrat Gazette. 1863.
Democratic Press. 1886.
True Democrat. 1861.

BOOKS

Abott, Grace, *The Child and the State*. 2 vols. New York: Greenwood Press, 1938.

Armor, William C., *Lives of the Governors of Pennsylvania*. Philadelphia: James K. Simon. 1873.

Bates, Samuel P., *Martial Deeds of Pennsylvania,*. Philadelphia: T.H. Davis. 1875.

Blackman, Emily C. *History of Susquehanna County*, Philadelphia: Claxon and Romson, 1873.

Boyer, Lee E., *The Story of Tressler Orphans Home*, Loysville: privately printed, 1931.

Bradley, Erwin, *The Triumph of Militant Republicanism*, Philadelphia: University of Pennsylvania Press, 1864.

Bremner, Robert H., *American Philanthropy*, Chicago: University of Chicago Press, 1960.

Bryce, Lord James, *American Commonwealth*, Edited by Louis Hacker, New York: G.F. Putman, 1959 (First published in 1888.)

Butler, Nicholas M., editor, *Education in the United States*, 2 vols., New York: J.B. Lyon, 1900.

Butts, N. Freeman and Laurence Cremin, *A History of Education in American Culture*, New York: Henry Holt, 1953.

Collins, Mary Ruth and Cindy F. Stauffer, *One Soldiers' Legacy: The National Homestead at Gettysburg, Gettysburg, PA*: Thomas Publications, 1993

Cremin, Lawrence A., editor, Horace Mann, *The Republic of the School*, New York: Teachers College Press. 1957.

Cubberley, Ellwood P. *Public Education in the United States*, New York: Houghton-Mifflin, 1947, revised edition.

Curti, Merle, *The Social Ideas of American Educators*, Patterson, N.J. : Littlefield,

Adams, 1965.

Davies, Wallace E. , *Patriotism on Parade: The Story of Veterans Organizations in America*. 1783-1900. Cambridge: Harvard University Press. 1955.

Davis, Stanton L. *Pennsylvania Politics*, 1860-1863. Cleveland: Western Reserve University Press, 1935.

Dearing, Mary R., *Veterans in Politics: The GAR*. Baton Rouge: Louisiana University Press, 1952.

Donehoo, George P. , *Pennsylvania. A History*, New York: Lewis Publishing Company, 1926.

Dunaway, Wayland, *History of Pennsylvania*. New York: Prentice – Hall,1948.

Dunkleman, Mark H., *Gettysburg's Unknown Soldier: The Life, Death and Celebrity of Amos Humiston*, Westport, Conn: Praeger, 1990

Egle, William H. , *Andrew Gregg Curtin*. Philadelphia: Avil Printing Company.1895.

Evans, Frank B. *Pennsylvania Politics, 1872-1877*, Harrisburg: Pennsylvania, Harrisburg: Pennsylvania Historical and Museum Commission, 1966.

Fine, Sydney, *Laissez-Farie and the General Welfare State*. Ann Arbor: University of Michigan Press 1956.

Fite, Emerson David. *Social and Industrial Conditions During the Civil War*, New York: Frederick Unger, 1963 (First published in 1910.)

Fletcher, Stevenson W., *Pennsylvania Agricultural and Country Life. 1840-1940*. Harrisburg: Pennsylvania Historical and Museum Commission. 1955.

Folks, Homer. *The Care of Destitute and Neglected Children*, New York: MacMillan, 1911.

Fortenbaugh, Robert, *Pennsylvania*, Harrisburg: Pennsylvania Book Service, 1940.

Friedlander, Walter A. *And Introduction to Social Welfare*, Prentice-Hall: Englewood Cliffs, NJ, 1861.

Garraty, John. *The American Nation*, New York: Harper and Row, 1966.

Garraty, John. *The New Commonwealth, 1877-1890*, New York: Harper and Row, 1968.

Ginger, Ray, *Age of Excess*, New York, MacMillan, 1965.

Glaab, Charles N. and A.T. Brown, *A History of Urban America*, New York: MacMillan, 1967.

Graham, Paul C., *History of the Indiana Soldiers' and Sailors' Orphan Home, 1865-1904*, Knightstown, Indiana: Home Journal, 1905.

Greene, Maxine, *The Public Schools and the Private Visions*. New York: Random House, 1965.

Hays, Samuel P., *The Response to Industrialism, 1885-1914*, Chicago, University of Chicago Press, 1957.

Heasseltine, William B., *Lincoln and the War Governors*, New York: Alfred P. Knopf, 1955.

Higginhotham, Sanford P. and W.A. Hunter, *Pennsylvania and the Civil War*, Harrisburg: Pennsylvania Historical and Museum Commission, 1961.

[no author], *History of Tioga County*, New York: W.S. Munsell, 1883.

Hughes, Edward W. And William C. McCracken, *The History of The Ohio Soldiers' and Sailors' Orphans Home*. Nania, Ohio: Association of Ex-Pupils. 1963.

Jenkins, Howard N., *Pennsylvania: Colinsland Federa. Vol III*. Philadelphia: Pennsylvania History Publishing Association, 1903.

Josephson, Matthew, *The Politicos*. New York: Harcourt, Brace, 1938.

Kamm, Samuel F. *The Civil War Career of Thomas A. Scott*, Philadelphia: University of Pennsylvania Press, 1940.

Katz, Michael B., *The Irony of Early School Reform*, Cambridge: Harvard University Press, 1968.

Lundberg, Emma O. , *Unto the Last of These*, New York: Appleton-Crofts, 1947.

McClure, Alexander K., *Old Time Notes of Pennsylvania*, Philadelphia: John C. Winston, 1905.

McClure, Alexander K., *The Life and Services of Andrew Gregg Curtin*, Harrisburg: Clarence M. Busch, 1855.

McKee, James A. , *History of Butler County*, Chicago: Richmond – Arnold, 1909.

McKelvey, Blake, *The Urbanization of America. 1860-1915*. New Brunswich: Rutgers University Press, 1963.

Meginnes, J.F. , *Biographical Annals of Lancaster County*, Lancaster: J.H. Beers, 1963.

Miles, Dudley, editor, *Philadelphia History of the Civil War*. Vol. N. New York: Thomas Yoseloff, 1957.

Mohr, Robert Landis, *Thomas Henry Burrowes*, Philadelphia: University of Pennsylvania Press, 1946.

Morgan, W. Wayne, editor, *The Gilded Age*, Syracuse: Syracuse University Press, 1963.

Mulhern, James, *History of Secondary Education in Pennsylvania*, Lancaster: Science Press, 1934.

Mylin, Amos, *State Prisons, Hospitals, Soldier Orphan Homes Controlled by the Commonwealth of Pennsylvania*, 2 vol., Harrisburg: Clarence S. Busch, 1897.

Paul, James Laughery, *Pennsylvania's Soldiers' Orphan Schools*, Philadelphia: Claxton and Remson, 1876.

Ripps, S. Alexander, *Educational Ideas In America*, New York: David McKay, 1969.

Riis, Jacob A., *How the Other Half Lives: Studies Among the Tenements of New York*, New York: C. Scribner's sons, 1890.

Schlesinger, Arthur M., *Rise of the City, 1878-1898*, New York: Macmillan, 1933.

Shimmell, L.S., *A History of Pennsylvania*, Harrisburg: R.L. Myers, 1890.

Stackpole, E.J., *Behind the Scenes With A Newspaper Man*, Philadelphia: J. B. Lippincott, 1927.

Stevens, Sylvester K, *Pennsylvania: Birthplace of the Nation*, New York: Random House, 1964.

Stevens, Sylvester K., *Pennsylvania: Heritage of A Commonwealth*, West Palm Beach: American History Company, 1968.

Stevens, Sylvester K., *The Keystone State*, New York: American History Company, 1956.

Stevens, Sylvester K., *Pennsylvania: The Titan Of Industry*, Vol I., New York: Lewsi Publishing Company, 1948.

Thatcher, Wallace L., *Harford Township*, (no publisher), 1940.

Thurston, Henry W., *The Dependent Child*, New York: Columbia University Press, 1930.

Walsh, Louise G. and Matthew J. Walsh, *History and Organization of Education in Pennsylvania*, Indiana: R.S. Groose, 1930.

Walter, Rush, *Popular Education and Democratic Thought in America*, New York: Columbia University Press, 1962

Wesley, Edgar S., *NEA: The First Hundred Years*, New York: Harper, 1957.

Wickersham, James Pyle, *A History of Education in Pennsylvania*, Lancaster: Inquirer Publishing Company, 1886.

Wiebe, Robert T., *The Search For Order, 1877-1920*, New York: Hill and Wang, 1967.

Yundt, Thomas H., *A History of the Bethany Orphans Home*, Reading: Daniel Miller, 1888.

Zeller, Bob, *The Blue and Grey in Black and White: A History of the Civil War in Photographs*, Praeger, 2005.

Monographs

Albright, Rebecca G., *"The Civil War Career of Andrew Gregg Curtin,"* Western Pennsylvania Historical Magazine, XLVII (October, 1964), 323-341; XLVIII (January, 1965), 18-42; XLVIII (April, 1965), 151-173.

Andrews, J. Cutler, *"The Gilded Age in Pennsylvania,"* Pennsylvania History, XXXIV (January, 1967), 9-25.

Bremner, Robert, *"The Impact of the Civil War on Philanthropy and Social Welfare, Civil War History,"* XII (December, 1966), 293-303.

The Gettysburg Examiner Magazine, May , 2014.

Gallarno, George, *"How Iowa Cared for Orphans of Her Soldiers of the Civil War,"* Annals of Iowa, 3rd series, XV (January, 1926), 163-193.

Heiges, George L., *"The Mt Joy Soldiers' Orphan School,"* Lancaster County Historical Society Papers, XLVIII (1944), 109-131.

Pierce, S.W., *"The Iowa Home for Soldiers' Orphans,"* Proceedings of the Sixth Annual Conference of Charities and Corrections, VI (1879), 153-155.

Stevens, Sylvester K., *"A Century of Industry in Pennsylvania"* Pennsylvania History, XXII (January, 1955), 49-68

Wiebe, Robert, *"The Social Functions of Education,"* American Quarterly, XXI (Summer, 1969), 148-167.

Unpublished Materials

Alanko, Tyyne, *"History of Soldiers' Orphan Institutions in Pennsylvania,"* Unpublished Master's Thesis, School of Social Service Administration, University of Chicago, 1933.

Baer, Lawrence, *"The Life and Educational Labors of James Pyle Wickersham,"* Unpublished Ph.D. Dissertation, University of Pittsburgh, 1939.

Flynn, Eleanor J., *"Public Care of Dependent Children in Pennsylvania,1676-1901,"* Unpublished Ph.D. Dissertation, University of Chicago, 1936.

Hefferan, Erma, *"A Little History of the Harford Soldiers' Orphan School,"* Susquehanna Historical Society (Typewritten)

McCoy, Eugene M. *"History and Development of the Pennsylvania Department of Public Instruction,"* Unpublished Ph.D. Dissertation, University of Pennsylvania, 1959.

Minute Book of the Mansfield Solders' Orphan School Association Gatherings, 1921-1935, In the possession of Elizabeth Allen, Mansfield.

Rathgeber, Lewis Wesley, *"The Democratic Party in Pennsylvania, 1880-1896,"* Unpublished Ph.D. Dissertation, University of Pittsburgh, 1955.

Scotland Veterans Childrens School, *"Post War Plans for Pennsylvania's Soldiers' Orphan School,"* no date or author (typewritten).

Scotland Veterans Children School, Folio-Scrapbok of the Scotland School containing newspaper clippings.

Interviews

Personal Interviews with Mr. Maurice Heckler, former assistant-principal of the Scotland School for Veterans Children, September 27, 1968.

Personal Interview with Mrs. Ida O'Brien, a former student at the Harford Soldiers' Orphan School, September 6, 1968.

INDEX

Key: S.O.S.= Soldiers' Orphan Schools of
Pennsylvania, 1864-1889

A

academies: become S.O.S., 50
academics favored over industrial studies: 115-116.
age differential in placement of children: 44-45.
agents used by owners to keep schools full: 132.
"The Alerts" baseball team: 80
Allen, F.A.: owner of Mansfield School and an innovator in teaching: 174-175.
allowance, clothing: 77.
almshouse: 178.
annual exam and graduation: 93-94
America Presbyter, The and the Gettysburg orphanage:193-196.
apprentice system: 112-113.
Attick, Mrs. inspector, on literary societies: 82.
automation as a problem of industrial education: 119

B

band, brass: 81
baseball: 80.
baths: 86.
Battle of Gettysburg: 191
Beaver, Governor James: champions industrial education: 122-123.
Bourns, Dr. James F. and the Gettysburg Homestead School for Soldiers' Orphans: 192-194; 198; 204-205; 208; 213-214; 222; 225; 228; 232; 242; 245.
breakfast: 62
brickmaking: 114.
broom making: 115; criticized by an orphan: 117.
buildings: 509-51; layout: 52;64;66.
burial sites: 181-182.
Burrowes, Thomas Henry: famous superintendent of the S.O.S.: 14-16; formulates age placement plan: 44-45; educational plan: 63-67; challenges Herbert Spencer: 71; on religious training: 74; on gambling: 81; inaugurates trips: 98;

speaks to the legislature: 89; favors academics: 116; victim of politics: 153; friend of Henry Barnard: 173-174.

"Buzzard, Abe": famous Lancaster County outlaw: 42

C

calisthenics for girls: 69-70, 76, 92; at exam: 94.
capitalistic tendencies: 128-129.
Carmichael, Rosa, "infamous matron" of the Gettysburg Homestead Orphanage: 204-205; 245-251; 228; 233; 235; 241-242; 246-248.
Cassidy, Lewis, Democratic Attorney-General and Pattison Investigation, 87; castigates the owners, 114; alleged to have gone on Pattison investigation to get favorable publicity for the coming gubernatorial campaign, 144; withdraws from the gubernatorial campaign, 147.
Cameron, Simon: 163.
character education stressed: 69-74.
Chester Springs: baseball team, 64; band: 81-82; literary society: 82; "run-aways": 84-85;
epidemics: 88; famous "flag pole" episode: 88; a Syndicate School: 135, 144; today: 1890-181.
"Children of the Battlefield" of Gettysburg: 191.,
chores: 115.
citizenship: 32; 68.
Clark, J.G. and his song, "Children of the Battlefield, written for the Gettysburg orphanage: 196-197.
clerks: 23-24: James L. Paul: 23-24.
class structure: 28-29.,
clothing: 77-79.
Commission replaces the Superintendency: 149.
Common School system: 175; 178.
communism and socialism, fear of: 111
"Copenhagen;" a boy's game.
corporal punishment: 83-84.
country side, rural location: 45-46.
Cooper, Thomas: 161-162.
crime: 30-32.
croquet: 81.
Curtin, Governor Andrew Gregg: first announcement of the S.O.S.: 6; address

to legislature, January, 1884: 186-188; Thanksgiving Day story: 8.

D

daily routine: 63-65.
Danville trip: 91
Dayton S.O.S.: 48-52.
Democratic Party of Pennsylvania: opposition to Governor Curtin: 9; York Democratic paper congratulates Curtin: 13; Democratic papers defend Governor Pattison: 160; Democrats do not press the "Scandal of 1886": 167-168.
denominations, religious: 74.
dental care: 88.
dependent care: 177.
dinner: 79.
discipline: 83
disease: 86
dominoes: 81
"Dotheboy's Hall": 102
dollars spent on the Schools: 185,
doctors: 88.

G

gambling: 81.
Gettysburg National Park: 20-23.
Governors of Pennsylvania: Curtin: 6-13; most are not involved with the S.O.S.: 13; Pattison: 157-160; Beaver: 122-123.
Grand Army of the Republic (GAR): interest in the S.O.S.: 38; pressure group: 38; outrage over "Scandal:" 103; Committee suggests changes: 172; joint committee with legislature: 173; GAR takes the lead in changing S.O.S.: 147-148; GOP charge the Democrats with trying to steal the GAR vote:166; GAR charge Rosa Carmichael of the Gettysburg Orphanage of misconduct: 245-246.
"Great Railway Strike of 1877": 111-112.
Guss, A.L.: S.O.S. owner: 153; his school closed: 156-157; accused of sexual improprieties: 153-156.

H

Harford S.O.S.: 47; today: 181.
Harrisburg trip: 88-90.
health: 86-88.

Higbee, Elnathan Elisha: last superintendent: 17; orphans to stay until adulthood: 34; on industrial education: 121-122; criticism of: 137-138; 143-144.

history teaching: 67-68

Humiston, Amos: Gettysburg battle death and origin of the Homestead Orphanage: 193-194; his wife, Philanda Humiston and her role in the Gettysburg Orphanage: 193-194; 197; 204.

"hunt the skipper" game: 80

Hutter, Elizabeth E: as the most interesting female inspector: 18-23; on the value of the S.O.S.: 34-35; dislike of labor unions: 111; as a Syndicate owner: 144-145.

I

industrial education: as a problem: 109; unsuccessful: 115-120; too expensive: 118.

Industrial Revolution: 108-109.

infirmary building: 87-88.

inspection, daily: 78.

Inspectors: 17-18; criticism of visits: 141; Governor Pattison is critical of: 141; Pattison fires: 147.

J

joint-stock company: 51.

L

labor unions: 111.

Ladies Aid: 3

Laws of Pennsylvania on S.O.S.: 35-37.

leadership of Pennslvania in establishing: 179.

"Leslie's Illustrated Newspaper" and the 1886 "Scandal:" 104.

library: 81

Lincoln, Abraham: friend of Hutter: 20-22; reference to by an orphan: 90

location: in rural areas: 45-47; difficulty getting to: 48-50.

logistics of the Philadelphia trip: 91.

Lunden family letters document the Gettysburg Homestead Orphanage: 205-244.

M

Mann, Horace on the need for social order: 41-42

Mansfield S.O.S.: 174-175; today: 184

matron: 55

McAlisterville S.O.S.: as a former academy: 50; A Syndicate school: 135; modern marker: 185; picture of today: 181.

McFarland, George: second superintendent: 17-18; on graded schools: 174

meals: 78-79.

Mercer S.O.S.: rural location: 46-47; a Syndicate school: 135; George Wright as owner: 135.

Michigan compared with Pennsylvania on care of soldiers' orphans: 179

Millersville State Normal School: 16.

military drill: 68-69; at exam time: 94; praise for: 99

Moore, Eleanore: as only female principal: 55-62.

moral conditions of entering orphans: 29

mothers: 47-48

Mt Joy S.O.S: 4th of July parade: 91; principal critical of industrial education: 115; a Syndicate school: 135; "skimping" on coffee: 137; today: 181.

music room: 81.

N

National Soldiers' Orphan Homestead Orphanage at Gettysburg: 197-204; end of: 249-250; para-normal tours today: 251.

National Teachers' Association: 16.

newspapers: praise of S.O.S.: 99-100; outrage over the "Scandal of 1886:" 103; critical of industrial education: 115; criticism of excessive profits: 131; outrage at Syndicate: 135; critical of inspectors: 141; happy about the end of the schools: 149.

newspaper, The Philadelphia Record's expose of the "Scandal": 101-102 night stools: 86.

Norris, John: Record reporter who broke the "Scandal": 102; accompanies Pattison investigation: 103.

Northern Home of Philadelphia: 5.

nurse: 88.

O

Ohio: second to Pennsylvania in care of soldiers' orphans: 179; acknowledges leadership of Pennsylvania: 179.

oral exam: 91.

origin of the S.O.S.: 6; first reference to: 6; address of Curtin, 1884: 186-188; Thanksgiving story: 8; Curtin as the prime mover: 13; legislature laws: 13;

orphanages: before the Civil War: 4; non-denominational: 4; for girls: 5; urban: 5' private: 5-6; S.O.S. are not to be orphanages: 44.

P

"pass and catch" game: 80.
Pattison, Governor Robert E,.: conducts investigation of the schools: 103; fires inspectors: 105; tries to dismiss Higbee: 105; political career in 1886 looks bright: 157; as a civil service reformer: 157; Higbee makes accusation against: 163-165; Republicans attack his investigation: 165.
Paul, James L.: as an inspector: 23-24; on social order: 42-43; charges against: 144; Democrats attack: 162.
Pearson, George: chief legislative clerk involved in Syndicate affairs and forced to resign post: 160-162.
pensions: 3.
Pennsylvania School Journal: 16; editor on Spencer and moral character: 69-71.
Pennsylvania State University: 16
Pennsylvania Railroad: grant to Curtin: 10-11; provides free trips for orphans: 88-91.
permanency of the schools as a problem: 119
Philadelphia: initial reference to meeting of 1863: 6; trip of orphans to: 91.
Philadelphia Record: breaks the "Scandal of 1886:" 102-103; accused by GOP of muckraking: 163.
physical condition of children at admission: 28-29.
playground: 80
playtime: 80.
political career of Governor Curtin: 8-9.
politics in Pennsylvania: public passion for: 151; officials of schools as political appointees: 153; factionalism: 153; Cassville school: 153-157; campaign of 1886 and Pattison: 157; two parties trade charges on condition of the schools: 159; GOP criticizes the Pattison investigation: 165; GOP accuses Democrats of trying to "steal" veterans' vote: 166; both parties back off "The Scandal:" 167.
praise from the press for the S.O.S.: 99-100.
principals of the schools: role of: 55; Eleanore Moore as only female principal: 55-62; diary of Mt. Joy principal on religious instruction: 74-75; criticism of industrial education: 115.
printing education for orphans: 114.
produce grown on schools' farms: 95.
profits: 129; Pattison investigation of: 131; Syndicate profits: 135; Higbee

criticizes: 137-138; newspapers criticize: 146.

Q

Quay, Matthew: state boss of GOP worried about the charges directed against "the Syndicate" in election of 1886, 142. questions asked at year-end oral examination, 78-79.

R

radicalism: 111.
recitation: by orphans to legislature in 1865: 89-90; a key educational concept: 64-65;
religious training: 74-75; denominations: 74.
reports: lacking in analysis: 25-27, 63; defend the schools: 38-39.
Republican Party: Chief Clerk Paul as a political appointee:23; accused by Democrats for the "Scandal of 1886:" 160; claim that the Philadelphia Record was a muckraking sheet: 163
run-aways: 84-85.
reunions: 170.
rural location: 45-46.

S

Sayers John: criticism as an inspector: 146.
"Scandal of 1886:" 97-107.
Scotland School for Soldiers'; Orphans: set up as a wholly owned state industrial school in 1893: 106 soldiers' orphans transferred: 124-126; closes in 2009: 180.
Scott, Thomas: president of the Pennsylvania Railroad grants funds to Curtin for S.O.S.: 10-11.
sewing machines used by girls to make clothing: 77
sexual misconduct charged against Cassville principal: 153-156.
shoe making as industrial education: 114.
singing by orphans to legislature in 1865: 89-90.
"skimping" by the owners on the children: 136-137.
social menace of the orphans: 28-29.
social order: as a key concern: 40-41.
soldier's home proposal: 11.
soldiers of the Civil War aided by Curtin: 12-13.
staff of the S.O.S.: 55.
states compared with Pennsylvania: 172; 179.
Superintendents: 14-17.

Spencer, Herbert: criticized by Wickersham: 71-72.
supper: 79
Syndicate schools: 135-139; Paul and Hutter as owners: 144; Legislative Clerk Pearson as an owner: 160-161; Senator Cooper as an owner: 162.

T

tailor: local makes the boys uniforms: 77.
teachers in the schools: 65.
Thanksgiving Day episode of Curtin: 8
trips of the orphans: to Harrisburg: 85; to Philadelphia: 91; at Mt. Joy: 91; to Danville: 91

W

Waters, A.H.: Uniontown principal as a businessman: 129.
Wagner, Lewis: new inspector in 1886 less favorable towards the owners: 140
Weaver, Charlie and his museum at Gettysburg: 250.
Wickersham, James Pyle: one of two famous super-intendents: 14-16; reports lack analysis: 25-26; on crime: 31-32; use of statistics: 34; on social order: 39; on military drill: 68-69; criticizes Spencer: 69-71; on moral education: 73; on need for industrial education: 109-110; on "pluck": 117; on use of agents: 132; on inspectors: 140; suffers because of political factionalism: 153; prepares a law setting up boarding schools for all dependent children of the state: 177-178.
making of wooden cabinets as industrial education: 114.
work details: for the girls: 95; for the boys: 95-96.
Wright, George: former state senator as leader of the Syndicate: 135; referred to as "shrewd and stingy:" 136-137; uses political influence to extend life of the S.O.S.: 160; newspapers urge him to come "clean:" 163.

Y

YMCA: 1

ABOUT THE AUTHOR

David Gold was born in the very, small hamlet of McEwensville, PA. His family moved to the nearby college town of Lewsiburg, PA where David attended the public schools and Bucknell University.

He served as a Navy musician in the Korean War.

Then, he returned to Bucknell and completed both his B.S. and M.S. degrees in History and Music.. But the most significant thing that took place during these years was the courting of his future wife, Barbara Grittner.

Next stop in his academic career was a two year appointment as a graduate assistant in history at the Pennsylvania State University.

This was followed by a long tenure as a high school teacher of history and philosophy in York, PA.

But his ultimate dream was to earn a Ph.D which he accomplished by 1971 when he earned the doctorate in the History and Philosophy of Education at the University of Maryland.

By now he had married Barbara and the two started raising a family- son, David and daughter, Martha

But, David continued teaching in high school as a Ph.D.

After his retirement, David wrote his first book: *The Gold Family History-Eleven Generations from Moravia to Pennsylvania.*

Presently, in his eighty's, he teaches philosophy to senior citizens in the OLLI program in York.